Being

Transfigured:

Lenten Homilies

CHRIS E.W. GREEN

Being Transfigured: Lenten Homilies

Chris E.W. Green

Copyright © 2023

Published by St. Macrina Press,
Abbotsford. BC
Printed in the United States
ISBN: 9798375021010

Bible Translations

NRSV: Revised Standard Version of the Bible, copyright © 1946, 1952, and 1971.
National Council of the Churches of Christ in the United States of America.
UBP. All rights reserved worldwide.
KJV: Public Domain

Cover Art:
"Christ is Creation" (2022): Chris E.W. Green
Cover Design: Bradley Jersak

St. Macrina Press

for +Ed

CONTENTS

A LENTEN PRAYER

Lord of Light, you have shown us that your glory rejoices to give us fullness of life; help us to know that our glory is the steadfast beholding of you, from whom all healing flows through Jesus Christ. Amen.

—Maggie Ross—

FOREWORD

Chris Green saw Jesus and didn't live to tell about it. These collected sermons are dispatches from the grave, where he lies buried with Christ (along with all those buried with him).

My friend Chris trusts that God is dead—really dead—and reminds those who have gotten behind Christ, those who follow him on the road to Golgotha, that by our baptism we join Jesus in his death.

Have you seen Hans Holbein's "Dead Christ"? If you stare at it long enough, a great hope takes hold. If you remain with Jesus in his death long enough, as Chris has, you begin to understand that stillness and weakness are the very conditions from which God makes all things new.

Divine helplessness is greater than any power in the cosmos and his death is at work in us and in the creation like leaven in bread, and the leaven turns out to be resurrection.

Here in the tomb of our shattered existence, where, dwelling among us, the human God has made his bed in hell, Jesus invites us to trust his wounds and his death, because the gospel is not first the news that we can receive Jesus into our lives; the gospel is first and foremost that Jesus has received us into his death.

All things must pass from death to life through his person, the One in whom nothing divine is absent, nothing human lacking. This person is whom you are going to experience as you read this book.

Read it slowly, like you have the kind of time someone whose life is buried with Jesus has. Contemplate silence and repentance, ponder doubt and identity as if the death of Jesus is your death because it is, and because it is, his kind of life is now your life.

And as you read you will find that God is at work in you. You will feel in your bones this wisdom from one of the first Christians: "What does it profit me to say that Christ has come to earth only in the flesh he received from Mary, if I do not show that he has also come in my flesh?" (Origen)

And this showing of Jesus in our flesh is not something for which we struggle, it is a grace, all of it a gift, for Christ is forever by the Spirit flesh of our flesh and bone of our bone, and we are crucified with him, are commended with Jesus into the Father's hands.

When we encounter Jesus Christ we don't live to tell about it. We die with him. And then we preach the sort of stories that follow, showing that by the weakness of his cross (and ours) joy has entered the world.

INTRODUCTION

I'm 5 years old, already a reader, tow-headed and bespeckled, wearing my father's white, V-neck T-shirt like a cassock, climbing into bed to read a bedtime story to my mother. I say to her with the purest confidence: "I'm going to be a preacher."

I've known since then this is work that I need to be doing.

It is difficult, risky work, of course. As Simon Tugwell, O.P., says, "Preaching is a dangerous occupation."
And not only for the hearers.
It is essential work, nonetheless.

For after that in the wisdom of God the world by wisdom knew not God, it pleased God by the foolishness of preaching to save them that believe. (1 Cor. 1:21)

I could've quoted that passage, at least the last line of it, the night I told my mother about my future.

†

Preaching *is* foolish. We all know that. It is foolish because we are speaking of and for *God*. It is foolish because *we* are speaking of and for God. It is foolish because we are *speaking* of and for God. But it's the kind of foolishness that God knows gets his Word said and done in the world.

So, we do it. Thankfully. Unpretentiously. Happily. Sure, preaching is foolish. But we are glad to play the fool—as Paul and his apostolic team were (1 Cor. 3:18).

I don't mean to suggest that the work of preaching is to be taken lightly. Not at all. I *do* mean to suggest that we can bear the weight of the burden only if we do not take ourselves too seriously.

I tried to get at the sense of playfulness I believe is essential to good preaching in a poem I wrote a few years ago—"In Defense of Crooked Preachers":

> Crooked preachers know what
> easy marks forget:
> > if God's corpse means anything it's that
> mercy hooks and yaws,
> reels and laps and
> gapes—breaking
> its own laws, bending us
> all all out of shape, so we
> never again dare speak for God—
> > at least not with a straight face.

Robert Jenson and Dietrich Bonhoeffer (Lutherans both) taught me this—preaching is not merely talking *about* what God has done or is going to do for us or to us. It's not simply restating, in our own words, "what the Bible says." Preaching, at heart, is not even merely an announcement of God's nearness given for the sake of exhorting or heartening, halting or healing our neighbors. No, preaching *is* that nearness.

A sermon does not merely say *that* Christ has died, Christ is risen, and Christ is coming again. It enters into and opens that mystery for us, making it so that *he* happens to us. In our preaching, Jesus speaks for himself—in the same voice that called the apostles and spoke through the prophets. And *his* word never returns void.

So, sermons, if they are not failed, "altar" us, fructifying in our deification. Like prayer, and as a form of prayer, preaching is participation in providence.

The Word words the world.

I was raised in a movement of street preachers and tent revivalists. I cut my teeth on sermons—*not* homilies!—that were, almost invariably, sweaty ordeals. Feats (if not also feasts) of endurance—for us, as well as for the preacher.

I cherish my birthright.

To this day, I am, unashamedly, a Pentecostal preacher. And precisely so, I am a sacramental and liturgical one. A sermon might break out anytime, anywhere—at the drop of a hat, my folk would say. But it makes its fullest sense in the church's gathered adoration and shared thanksgiving around the Lord's Table.

I've come to believe that Christian worship, *Pentecostal* worship, is essentially Eucharistic. And I'm convinced that the sermon is essential to our worship because it is the way the Spirit prepares us to receive Christ's body and blood and to feed on him in our hearts by faith.

Given that that is true, we might describe the relationship between Word and Sacrament something like this: the sermon, given and received, is the inspired and en-Spirit-ed intelligibility of the Eucharist, arousing our longing for God, our desire for communion with the Word; the Eucharistic celebration just *is* that communion, the mystery of our being given by God to us in the very gifts of bread and wine we have offered to him with our thanks. Remember, at the Transfiguration, recalling the events of the Baptism, the Spirit falls and rests on the *body* of the Son, and the Father says, "This is my beloved Son... *Listen* to him!" There, then, as in our weekly gathering, the Body is given to the apostolic community in a call to hear the Word.

I've dedicated this book to my bishop, Edwin Rodriguez-Gungor, because he, more than anyone else, has helped me to understand where my preaching belongs.

These homilies were given in 2021. I followed the readings from the Revised Common Lectionary (Year B). I shared a version of the series at that time in Macrina Magazine. They've been substantially edited, updated, and reworked—read: made unbearably longer—for this publication.

Thanks to Micah Enns and Macrina Magazine for agreeing to publish these sermons then, and thanks to Bradley Jersak for insisting I reshape them and publish them now in this new form. Bradley also designed the book's cover, which I love. (I'm hoping in this case that you'll break the old rule against judging books by their covers.)

Thanks, too, to Mario Hood for his guidance and encouragement, and Michael Austin Kamenicky for his edits. Without their interventions, this book wouldn't have happened at all, or, worse, would've been a complete mess.(If you find errors, blame Austin.)

Finally, I owe a special thanks to Fr Kenneth Tanner. I'm glad to have written this book if only because it forced him to write that foreword.

✝

"In closing," as we preachers say, let me offer an encouraging word about how preaching embodies the strange light of Lent.

Tugwell, a Catholic charismatic and Dominican friar, opens *The Way of the Preacher* by identifying the preacher as "a bearer of the Word of God... entrusted by God with his Word for others." He urges us to feel the work of preaching as the work of *beholding God*. In his words, preaching is "a truly contemplative way of life," an occasion for and means of coming into conscious awareness of our union with God.

Tugwell also insists that our humanity, even in its fallenness, is not something God has to "fix" in order to make himself heard in our words. Indeed, "our own confused human experience," he says, "is the stuff out of which God is making a face and a word for himself, to clothe him who is his Face and Word."

> It is our flesh, our humanity, that the divine Word took in Mary, and it is our flesh still, our humanity, that he takes day by day to be his Body, the garment of his glory.

George Herbert's "The Windows" puts it unforgettably: the preacher's humanity is " a brittle crazie glasse." When God's light shines through the glass—the glass of being, the glass of presence, the glass of words—a window is made. The light makes the window. The window does not make the light. But the window does, because of its stains and craziness, not in spite of them, give the light a particular shine.

The poem's second stanza makes clear that God's story is "annealed in glass"—meaning that the preacher, and each of her sermons, must be exposed again and again to the fire of God—and then given time to cool, to cure. Apart from that tempering, she and whatever she says will prove to be "waterish, bleak, and thin."

That said, Updike's preacher is not quite right. Our job as preachers is *not* to burn our hearers with the ferocity of our belief. The light of God does what it does whether we are "hot" with Christ or not. What matters, when all is said and done, is not my making my faith powerful, but God's brilliance working in my darkness. That is why we "crazie," "brittle" preachers preach—even when we're not "feeling it."

"Advent begins in the dark." Fleming Rutledge tells us that. Epiphany, climaxing in the Transfiguration, allows us to enter into the even deeper dark of Lent, a darkness not only of hope but also of *love*, darkness pregnant with uncreated light.

Knowing that, knowing it against knowing, which is the only way we can know it now, we can see Lent not so much as a season for discipline as a season for transfiguration, a time for letting ourselves be illumined once again by the hope for God and neighbor created through the love of the Gospel.

The light of that hope, fired by love, the light which shines not only on Tabor but also on Golgotha, shows us the truth of our being. And in that light, we see light—and shine with it.

A final note: there are seven sermons in this series, the first for the last Sunday of Epiphany and the last for Palm Sunday. I've arranged the chapters so there are forty separate passages, set off by this mark: ✝. That way it can be used as a daily devotional. The book does not have to be read that way, of course. You should read it as you feel led or see fit.

1

Transfiguring Silence

A Sermon for the Last Sunday after Epiphany

2 Kings 2:1-12; Psalm 50:1-6; 2 Corinthians 4:3-6; Mark 9:2-9

Today, at the threshold between Epiphany and Lent, the Scriptures, as always, turn our attention once again toward Jesus, urging us not merely to look at him but to listen to him as he is transfigured for and before us.

The Psalm (Ps. 50:1-6) celebrates creation as the goodness that exists because God has spoken about it and to it. And it assures us that when God comes to speak the final word, the Word that he is, the Word that will be the Last Judgment, he will come wrapped in the wind and flame that attended his appearances to Moses and Elijah.

The reading from the Old Testament allows us to hear Elisha, Elijah's successor to-be, hushing the sons of the prophets who've crowded like pundits or paparazzi around the unfolding events: "Yes, I know the Lord will take my master away from me today. Keep quiet" (2 Kgs. 2:1-12). Once they're silenced, we see Elisha as he watches his father, Elijah, ascend into heaven in a chariot of fire, translated up into the future he sees God intends for us all.

The New Testament reading, drawn from St Paul's second letter to the Corinthians, shows us Jesus' face—shining, even in death, with God's unapproachable light. Then it presses us to remember that we can recognize this Galilean as God only because the Creator Spirit has spoken that vision into being for us. The apostle's claim is stupendous: the very God who in

the beginning said, "Let there be light" now dwells
within and among us, illumining us from within with
"the light of the knowledge of the glory of God" that
rays out from the countenance of the crucified (2 Cor.
4:3-6). The crucified one is, we confess, God from
God, true light from true light. In him, the light that is
our life came into being (Jn 1:3-4). Thus, he is in us the
light of the world.

The Gospel, as I said, makes us first-hand witnesses of
Christ's transfiguration. And it assures us that we are
meant to suffer the same conversion Peter, James, and
John had to undergo. It also leaves us with a warning:
there are dangers in being exposed to God.

All these readings, taken together, and seen in the light
of the Gospel's searing promise, bear witness to our
one hope. This is it: as we are given to *behold* God in
Christ, we cannot help but begin to *hold* his likeness.

Looking to him, listening to him, we begin, thank God,
to look and sound more and more like Jesus, to move
as he moves, to see as we are seen and to hear as we are

3

heard. That hope, the hope of our transfiguration, the hope of holding what we are beholding, is what Hebrews calls the "better hope" (Heb. 7:19), the "sure and steadfast anchor of the soul" (Heb. 6:19).

✝

As St Mark tells the story, Peter, James, and John ascend a "high mountain apart" with Jesus, no doubt to pray with him. Suddenly, Jesus is "transfigured before them."

In spite of the way it's often represented to us, this was not a mere curiosity or even a spectacle. St Thomas Aquinas says that the glory of Jesus' soul suddenly, miraculously, poured out into his body and overflowed it, revealing his divinity. In the words of St John of Damascus:

> Christ is transfigured, not by putting on some quality he did not possess previously, nor by changing into something he never was before, but by revealing to his disciples what he truly

was, in opening their eyes and in giving sight to those who were blind. For while remaining identical to what he had been before, he appeared to the disciples in his splendor; he is indeed the true light, the radiance of glory.

He is the *true* light.

He is the true light.

He *is* the true light.

The glory shining out from Jesus was not light as we know it, but that which light represents and signifies by participation in that which we do not and cannot yet know: the invisible, unapproachable, uncreated reality of the divine life.

When we confess that Jesus is "God from God, light from light," we are not speaking of electromagnetic waves. We are speaking, instead, of God's "essence"— how it is that God is God. St Gregory Palamas, the 14th century bishop and hesychastic theologian, frames it like this:

hesychastic: contemplative monastic tradition in the eastern Christian tradition in which stillness is sought through uninterrupted Jesus prayer.

5

This mysterious light, inaccessible, immaterial, uncreated, deifying, eternal, this radiance of the Divine Nature, this glory of the divinity, this beauty of the heavenly kingdom, is at once accessible to sense perception and yet transcends it.

So, when we say Christ was "transfigured," we mean there was, for a moment, a perfect *clarity* to his being. Suddenly, Peter, James, and John saw him—clearly—in his fullness. Or, better, they saw for a moment the signs of sheer, unconditional otherness. Jesus' clothes became as revelatory as his face.

They also saw the signs of their reality altering around him. And Israel's great dead and gone prophets, Elijah and Moses, are suddenly, magnificently alive and present, talking with Jesus about the suffering that awaits him, readying him for his exodus and remembering how he had led them through their own.

The apostles are wholly overwhelmed.

As the Gospel makes clear, Peter, James, and John are not impressed or curious—they are *terrified*. Why? Because, as Maximus the Confessor says, the light from the face of Jesus had "conquered their blessedness."

Later, the apostles will recall this as the defining experience of their lives (2 Pet. 1:16-18). But in the heat of that moment, as it was unfolding, as it fell on them, as they were taken up into it, Christ's transfiguration carried them to the very edge of the very edge of their being. James and John are left speechless. Peter, afraid not only for himself but also for his friends, cannot keep from speaking.

Strikingly, at the end of Mark's Gospel, three women—Mary Magdalene, Mary the mother of James, and Salome—come to Jesus' tomb to anoint his body. To their surprise, when they arrive, the stone has already been moved, and an angel declares the good news to them: Jesus has risen from the dead and they are to go and tell the disciples—Peter, in particular—that they are to meet him in Galilee. Like the apostles on the mountain, the women are overcome by their experience in the garden: "So they went out and fled from the tomb, for terror and amazement had seized them; and they said nothing to anyone, for they were afraid" (Mk. 16:8).

We should take a moment to feel the cumulative weight of these stories. To let the shock of it wash over us. Peter, James, and John see Jesus as he is—and it is too much for them. Mary, Mary, and Salome see not Jesus but the absence his presence has made—and it is too much for them.

In each case, what is seen is alarming, throwing the disciples into panic. They have come up hard against the edge of their being, the end of themselves. Peter speaks—because he wants to interrupt what is happening. Mary Magdalene finds she cannot speak—because she cannot handle the interruption that is happening.

Like them, we want what *we* want. And like them, we fear the "too-muchness" of God. How could we not?

We do not know how to live into a future, even the one God promises, if it overturns our past completely. How could we? We want God to secure our standing— without turning our world entirely upside down. We want change and to be changed. We do not want to die. And that is why we need to move from Epiphany into Lent.

☩

When Peter interrupts, offering to build three tabernacles, neither Jesus nor Elijah nor Moses responds to him. Instead, a cloud—*the* cloud, the Cloud of the Presence, which led Israel through the wilderness day by day—appears and covers them. Why? Because Peter and the other apostles could not take in the uncreated light. God, therefore, embraces them in his creative darkness.

In that darkness, seeing nothing, they finally hear the Father's voice: "This is my Son, the Beloved; listen to him!" To their surprise, however, they hear—nothing from Jesus. They see him, now alone, and he does not say a word. For a while they are left, as Moses and Elijah had been, with nothing but the sound of silence.

Jesus does not speak until they begin to descend the mountain. And when he finally does speak, he offers no explanation, no reassurance. He simply prohibits them from sharing their experience: "Do not tell anyone what you have seen, until after the Son of Man has been raised from the dead."

What does this mean for us? Why has the Spirit told these stories in these ways? Because we, like the first disciples, tend to speak up when we should quiet down, and quiet down when we should speak up. Life and death, Scripture says, are in the tongue. But only the Spirit can teach us to speak life and death *as the Father speaks them*—as they are embodied in the Son.

In *Life Together*, Dietrich Bonhoeffer argues that we cannot speak the Gospel to others until we have learned to hold our tongues. This is especially true, he says, when what occurs to us to say seems obviously right—as what they said must have seemed right to the sons of the prophets around Elisha and the friends around Job. Sometimes, what others need most is for us not to say a word.

I don't mean to sound cynical, but I think we've convinced ourselves that feeling strongly about something gives us all the permission we need to say whatever, whenever, however we like. But the Spirit of life, the Spirit of truth, teaches us otherwise.

If the truth is not known in love, if it is not held in intercession and compassion, if it is not offered in courage and humility, then what we know is not the truth at all. So, we have to learn to reign in our thoughts, to hold our tongues. As Bonhoeffer says, it is only out of that discipline and the meekness it forms in us that all true ministry comes—listening, bearing, helping, and proclaiming.

God wants for us more than the silence of negation, of course. He sometimes embraces us, as he embraced the apostles on Mt Tabor, in the cloud of unknowing. He does this because we, like Peter and Mary and the other first witnesses, need time to take in what we have seen and heard, to comprehend what has comprehended us.

Lent affords us this time, preparing us for the unbearable darkness of Good Friday and the unapproachable light of Easter. If the Epiphany of the one we longed for in Advent "conquers our blessedness," then Lent teaches us how that defeat is a blessing. As we learn to accept our limits as graced, we find ourselves opened wider and wider to the uncreated light, the glory of God's own inner life. To be silenced by God is to be impregnated with the Word. To be enfolded in God's darkness is to be enlightened with the uncreated light.

In her book, *A Short and Easy Method of Prayer* (which, alas, landed her in prison as a suspected heretic), Jeanne Guyon says that "inner silence" is necessary for receiving the fullness of God. This becomes possible, she says, only through the long-term practice of "outer silence." Over time, thanks to the Spirit, we learn "recollection" and "retirement," developing the skills and disposition necessary to unbusy ourselves, to quit thinking about what our "flesh" feels as pressing, and to gather our attention, scattered in all directions by the cares of the day, toward God. As we do this, Guyon assures us, God is granted access to the roots of our being, to the heart of our heart, working in us far below the level of our awareness, always closer to us than we are to ourselves, doing what only he can do—healing what we did not even know had been wounded, filling us up with eternally abundant life.

"The Lord is in his holy temple; let all the earth keep silence before him" (Hab. 2:20). In Lent, as in Advent, we learn to practice silence —and to practice it *before God*.

We relinquish our fixed ideals and suspend our judgments, unclenching our fists so we can receive the gifts of God. We are, as Bonhoeffer says, silent for the sake of listening: "Silence ultimately means nothing but waiting for God's word."

This kind of silence, born out of respect for the otherness of God and sustained by our gratitude for Jesus, slowly attunes us to the world the Father knows and makes known through the Spirit. The more attuned we become to *that* reality, the more capable we are of loving as we have been loved. In ways we can never quite explain, we begin to notice, even if only fleetingly, what had before always escaped our attention. And more and more we find we are better able to give our attention to others—rather than having to have it captivated.

Lent, as we all know, is a time of repentance, contrition, and atonement. A time of discipline, sacrifice, and self-denial. But all of that is intended to sensitize us to the delicate movements of grace within and among and around us, the almost-imperceptible after-effects of Epiphany.

We keep silence so the still, small voice can be heard.

For God, of course, both silence and speech are Word. As we learn to listen, more and more fully, both to what God is saying and is not saying, we not only come to know God as he is and others as they are, but also to know ourselves as we are. Most mysteriously of all, we come to be known exactly as we *need* to be known.

Once, while Julie and I were at lunch, we could not help but overhear a conversation between two young women seated across the room from us. It was not quite a *conversation*. One of the two women was allowed to speak only twice. She was able to ask exactly two one-line questions. Both times her friend interrupted before she could finish the line.

Afterward, on our way home, I said something about how desperately that woman, the one who did all the talking, the one who couldn't let her friend even ask a question, needed to be known. Julie agreed, but recognized something I had overlooked entirely. It was precisely her endless talking that kept her from being known. Like all of us at one time or another, she simply could not be quiet long enough to be heard.

That touches the nerve of the mystery, doesn't it? We are most fully known not when we say everything we think, but when we listen most attentively. Not when we bare our souls, but when we bear others' burdens. Maggie Ross has it exactly right:

> There is a hidden glory radiating from each person which will reveal itself only to those who have been able to focus outward and wait in generosity, thus allowing their own hidden glory—hidden especially from themselves—to pour forth.

Peter, fearing that the uncreated light will reduce him and his world to dust and ashes, wants to *make*—to build familiar structures, to establish frameworks he knows how to use. And he tries to use his words to accomplish this making. But God's word does not make—it *creates*. And that creativity, as we experience it, threatens to *unmake* so much we have been made to think we need.

Like Peter, James, and John, like Mary, Mary, and Salome, we need the Spirit to lift the veil from our eyes, to overshadow us with the cloud of divine darkness, so we can begin to discern the difference between making something for ourselves—something familiar, useful, and safe—and creating something for others— something better than we or they could have known even to desire.

We need to know this difference between making and creating. And our neighbors, including our family and our friends, as well as our enemies and whatever strangers we happen to meet, need us to know it. The last thing they need is for us to do what Peter thought needed to be done—to make tabernacles for them or to build shrines to them. No, they need exactly what we need: to be seen and to be heard—sympathetically, clearly, and fully. In other words, they need us to see them, to recognize them as Christ's just as we recognize Christ as God's. They need us to see the light of the knowledge of the glory of God shining on *their* faces.

We need to know that God is at work in them in ways beyond our imagination or control. We need to know that God already tabernacles in them for us, speaking in their words and drawing near in their presence. And they need to know that we know this. They need to feel our delight in that knowing. If we can see how this is true of them because it is true of Jesus, then we will also see it is true of us, and for the very same reason.

C.S. Lewis, famously, ended his "Weight of Glory" sermon by reminding his hearers that "next to the Blessed Sacrament, your neighbor is the holiest object presented to your senses." But the truth, believe it or not, is far, far, far more mysterious—

2

Transfiguring
Death

A Sermon for the First Sunday in Lent
Genesis 9:8-17; Psalm 25:1-9; 1 Peter 3:18-22; Mark 1:9-15

Unlike the other Evangelists, Mark recounts Jesus' baptism and his temptation as one story, not two. And he tells it in a single breath—forcing us to witness these experiences both-at-once as twinned movements in the unfolding of a single event.

Half-awed, half-horrified, we watch as Jesus is driven out into the wilderness with his clothes still sopping and the divine blessing still ringing in his ears. The temptation he undergoes is not described. He suffers it alone. We see him, but only in the distance. And we hear nothing. We're told that he is with the wild beasts, and that when his trial is finished, angels minister to him.

Once we've caught our breath, we find that the details of Mark's account, quick as they are, call up for us the defining moments of Israel's past. The Exodus and the Wandering, obviously, but also the Conquest, the Kingdoms, and the Exile. According to Mark, Jesus re-lives these defining moments in ways both like and unlike his fathers and mothers.

In his baptism, Jesus does not pass through on dry ground as Moses and Joshua had done. He descends, instead, into the muddy depths, going down with Pharaoh and his armies, damned with the damned. Rising from the waters under the rent heavens, he does not exult or celebrate as his mother Miriam and the daughters of Israel had celebrated. Instead, in solidarity with the Canaanites, he is driven out from the Promised Land into the wild wastes. There, in the throes of his conflict with the Enemy, he does what even David could not. He resists evil without violence, without bloodshed, and truly defeats it.

In these and other ways, Mark's Gospel shows us how Jesus, as Israel's promised prophet, priest, and king, enters into our existence so completely, so unconditionally, that his reality and ours become mutually determinative. Thanks to that bond, which the Spirit creates, what happens to us happens in him, and what happens in him happens to us. As St. Athanasius said, the Word (becomingly!) became what we are so that we might become what he is.

As we move through this Lenten season, we should remember not so much that we are mortal as that we share in *God's* mortality. St Paul was deadly serious when he said Christ's death lives in us for sake of the life of the world (2 Cor. 4:7-12).

And we should remember not so much that we are tempted but that our temptations take place with and within *God's* temptations.

Talk of God's temptations and God's mortality may strike you as strange. But it's ancient wisdom, the teaching of the church's Fathers and Mothers. They tell us that Jesus was baptized not to wash away his sins but to sanctify the waters. In the same way, he was tempted not to prove his sinlessness but to hallow the wilderness.

Jenson taught me to say it like this: Jesus does not suffer the fact that he suffers. He suffered—and suffers—actively, transfiguringly. Nothing from his birth to his death happened to him but what his Father wanted to happen differently for us. Whatever he underwent, he changed for our sakes. And he changed it, so to speak, from the *inside*. St Ephrem says in one of his hymns on the church that Moses' brightness came on him from without, but the Jordan, like Mary, was baptized by light from within. That's God's way.

In the end, what happened to Mary, God's mother, and to the Jordan, God's river, happened to life itself—because it happened first to death.

✝

The forty days, the water, the dove, the angels, the wild beasts, the judgment of God—these details draw our attention to the story of Noah, a story that takes us back behind the stories of Abraham, Moses, David, and Elijah, back to the beginning that made Israel's election necessary. And this story, which Jesus re-enacts in his baptism/temptation, both plots for us the risks inherent in being God's people and doing God's work, and casts a vision of the life lived faithfully to the end, a life made possible by the love of the God who raises the dead but does not keep us from dying.

When Noah is first introduced (in Genesis 6), he is likened to Abel: he finds favor in God's eyes because he is righteous, blameless, and faithful. After the flood, as soon as he steps from the ark, he builds an altar and his sacrifices are said to be pleasing to God, as Abel's

23

had been. But then, abruptly, Noah is likened to *Cain*. Without explanation, he is said to be, exactly as Cain was, "a man of the soil." After he drinks some of the wine from his vineyard, Noah is left "uncovered" in his tent—naked and ashamed, like Adam after the Fall.

What are we to make of this sudden ruin?

If Noah was righteous and blameless and faithful before the flood, and if after the flood the earth had been renewed, freed from the wicked and their wickedness, how does he fall into sin? How does anyone who for so long lived like Abel suddenly turn out to be like Cain? Especially in a new Eden?

We should not be surprised by how Noah's story ends. We would not be if we were as familiar with these texts as we're tempted to think we are. For whatever reason, however, it seems the more we've praised the virtues of the Bible and insisted on its authority, the less we've given the Scriptures the careful, discerning attention they demand.

As a result, we've tended to convince ourselves that we know the sacred texts much better than we actually do. So, in spite of the fact that we're familiar with the story of Noah's ark—or, better, precisely because of *how* we are familiar with it—we do not know the arc of Noah's story. And the same goes for more or less all the stories in the sacred texts.

The parable of the prodigal son, for example, is not a story of restoration and reconciliation. In spite of the way we read it, it does not end happily. In the end, the sons are even more estranged from each other and from their father than they were in the beginning. And this same sad pattern appears again and again in Scripture.

Abraham spends the last years of his life estranged from all his children, including Isaac. Moses, after everything, is kept from entering the Promised Land. David dies in bitterness, his family shattered, his nation at war, his mouth filled with curses. Solomon receives the wisdom he asks from God, but allows it to lead him into misery and despair. Elijah confronts the false prophets and calls fire down from heaven, only to find that it makes no difference at all to anyone.

Even God's own works seem not to matter, at least his works of judgment. He consumes Sodom and Gomorrah in the fires of judgment; but while the smoke still rises from the plain, Lot's daughters rape their father. God opens up the earth to swallow Korah and the others who rebelled, but the following morning the entire nation rebels against Moses and Aaron.

Why do we misread these stories so badly? Why can't we follow their arcs to their ends? Ultimately, because we haven't yet learned to read *Jesus'* story faithfully. We almost invariably read his story so that it ends on Easter, not Good Friday.

I suspect we insist on reading it this way because we want (unconsciously, of course) his death to be felt as only a temporary interruption in the flow of his life. Whether we can admit it to ourselves or not, we want to speak of his death in ways that allow us to think optimistically about our future. "It's Friday," we say, "but Sunday's coming."

This misreading of his story allows us to feel a kind of comfort—as if we might survive our deaths as he survived his, as if the arc of history bends toward justice. But all that is wishful, magical thinking. It has nothing to do with the hope of the Gospel.

✝

Not long ago, someone asked me what I thought Jesus was doing while he was dead. I knew what the questioner expected me to say, of course. I knew the answer he wanted to hear. But the right answer is that Jesus wasn't doing anything while he was dead. That's what it means to say he was dead!

He was *crucified*. He *died*. He *was buried*.

"What is not assumed is not healed." That includes dying and being dead. It is good that Jesus did not merely seem to die. We confess it week after week: he died; he was buried; he descended into hell. Jesus did not survive his death. He did not go on with his saving work "in the spirit realm" while his body lay in the ground. He was, in the language of the Psalm, "forsaken among the dead" (Ps. 88:5).

What is more, Jesus *feared* death—and not without reason. In the garden, he cried out "to the one who was able to save him from death" (Heb. 5:7). And he was heard! We know he was heard because he was not kept from dying but was kept in death—so that he might be dead with the dead, and so they might be raised from death with him.

We need to face these facts. And we also need to face the even harder truth: Jesus' life did not end happily. He died gracefully, to be sure. But he also died in agony, mostly forsaken by those he loved. So far as anyone could see, he died a failure.

We do believe, of course, that he rose from the dead on the third day! But we do *not* believe that he "came back to life." His death was final, conclusive, definitive—as yours will be, and mine. Yes, as today's Epistle says, "He was put to death in the flesh, but made alive in the Spirit." The making alive, however, did not follow the putting to death as one damned thing follows another. When we speak of resurrection, we're not speaking about "the next thing" that happened to Jesus after he died.

Death and resurrection are not two points on the same timeline. No, when we speak of resurrection, we're referring to something that happened to Jesus in his fullness. And that fullness necessarily includes the end of his life, the completion of his work. To confess that Christ has died and that Christ is risen is to confess that his *entire life*, including his dying and his being dead, has been taken up into God as the source, guide, and goal of all things. Raised from the dead, the entirety of his life, including his death, was revealed in its fullness as the life of God with us and for us. Theologically speaking, therefore, Sunday does not follow Friday; it *fulfills* it.

✝

Jesus' arc is different from Noah's and Abraham's and David's and Solomon's and Elijah's not only because he remained faithful to the end, but also because he remained faithful to the end for their sake and ours. That is why his life is *the* Ark, the only vessel in which Noah and Abraham and David and Solomon and Elijah—and everyone and everything else, besides—can be borne through death into God.

Karl Rahner saw this clearly:

> Jesus has accepted death. Therefore, this must be more than merely a descent into empty meaninglessness. He has accepted the state of being forsaken. Therefore, the overpowering sense of loneliness must still contain hidden within itself the promise of God's blessed nearness. He has accepted total failure. Therefore, defeat can be a victory. He has accepted abandonment by God. Therefore, God is near even when we believe ourselves to

have been abandoned by him. He has accepted all things. Therefore, all things are redeemed.

As St Paul says, nothing can separate me from the love of God. Why? Because, and only because, God has already taken even the experience of separation as his own. He has descended to the depths, claiming even the lowest lows of hell. "The death he died, he died ... once for all" (Rom. 6:11). "One has died for all; therefore, all have died (2 Cor. 5:14).

I learned this song when I was a child: "Because he lives, I can face tomorrow; because he lives, all fear is gone." But it is closer to the truth to say that I can face tomorrow because he *died*.

Yes, he lives! But not in the sense that he survived his death. The crucifix does not lie. He did not escape death; he led captivity itself captive. And he did so precisely by accepting the finality of death, yielding up his life to God in such a way that death itself died and his death was made alive.

Believe it or not, it is precisely in his death that he harrows hell. As with us, so with him. God's strength is made perfect in weakness and God's life is manifested in death.

Jesus is worshipped as "more than a conqueror" because he triumphed in his defeat. Dead, capable of nothing, he accomplished everything. And is this not the truth of my baptism, the truth I pray I do not forget in my temptations?

My life is his because his death is mine. I share God's mortality. In his death I live and move and have my being. And because he died, once for all, life is worth the living—even if not all the fear is gone.

3

Transfiguring Identity

A Sermon for the Second Sunday in Lent
Genesis 17:1-7; Psalm 22:22-30; Romans 4:13-25; Mark 8:31-38

F ollowing the arc of the Christian year—Sunday to Sunday, season to season—we follow the disciples as they follow Jesus. Eventually, it begins to dawn on us: what's happening to them is happening to us, and we can no longer tell where exactly their story ends and ours begins. As St Paul says, the words of God witnessed in Scripture were written for our sake too (Rom. 4:23-24).

Two weeks ago, at the threshold between Epiphany and Lent (every threshold is a threshing floor), we saw him, as they did, transfigured on the mountain. And with them we heard the Father avow him as Beloved.

Last week, the first Sunday in Lent, we saw him baptized in the river and tempted in the wilderness. And, once again, we heard the Father's avowal.

This week, we watch as Peter takes Jesus by the lapels and dresses him down for his foolishness.

It's shocking, even if we know it's coming. And it's all the more shocking in the light of what we know has just happened. In the immediately preceding passage, Jesus asks about the word on the street. The report, which we overheard, is amusing, but telling. Jesus is seen by the crowds as forbidding and troublesome—a new Elijah, perhaps; or, worse, John the Baptist reborn. When Jesus asks the Twelve what they think about what they've heard, they fall silent. All except you-know-who.

In Matthew's Gospel, Peter's answer is explosive: "You are the Christ! The Son of the living God!" (Mt. 16:16). Jesus responds with delight and blessing, entrusting him with the mysteries and giving him the name, "Peter," which lays the groundwork for the church's future.

But in Mark's Gospel, Peter's confession is terse, to-the-point. And Jesus responds only by warning the disciples not to tell anyone about what they now know. Immediately after that warning, however, Jesus begins for the first time to speak openly with them about his mission:

> Jesus began to teach his disciples that the Son of Man must undergo great suffering, and be rejected by the elders, the chief priests, and the scribes, and be killed, and after three days rise again. (Mk. 8:31).

Up to this point in the Gospel, Jesus has been guarded, insisting that his identity must be kept secret. Now, he speaks "quite openly" (Mk. 8:32a). As soon as the secret is unveiled, Peter snaps. He tries to take Jesus in hand, to drag him back in line. Mark's account is as sharp as it is quick: "And Peter took him aside and began to rebuke him" (Mk. 8:32b).

Peter takes Jesus aside.

Let those words sink in. The moment Peter realizes what Jesus intends, he comes apart. He panics. And in his panic, he tries to take *Jesus* apart. He takes Jesus aside trying to find a side of Jesus he can reason with and appeal to, a side of Jesus that answers to his own preferred self-image. Mark says that Peter "rebukes" Jesus, as Jesus earlier had rebuked the unclean spirit (Mk. 1:25) and the storm (Mk. 4:39). Actually, more to the point, Mark says "he *began* to rebuke him."

How does this happen? And why? It is easy to caricature this exchange. Peter does make a fool of himself. And yet... It is all too easy to imagine his rebuke as pompous and paternalistic. I suspect it was earnest and sympathetic, born not of conceit but of misguided compassion. Perhaps, deep down in his bones, Peter sensed something of the weight of Gethsemane and Golgotha, and knew, in a flash, that it would crush them all. Perhaps he saw the shadow of the darkness of that mystery pass over Jesus' face and could not help but try to save his friend.

Regardless, Jesus interrupts Peter's rebuke, right at the start, with a rebuke of his own: "Get behind me, Satan! For you are setting your mind not on divine things but on human things" (Mk. 8:33).

In spite of what some have said, Jesus does not name Peter "Satan." He does not level an accusation at him. That would be to do the Devil's work for him, and Jesus never does that. No, Jesus names *for* Peter what is happening in and through him—so he can be free of it. And he reminds Peter of his place as a disciple: "Get behind me" (Mk. 8:33).

Jesus does this, Mark says, after turning to look at the disciples. These are not meaningless details. (There are no meaningless details in any passage of Scripture.) They recall the earlier story of the hemorrhaging woman who pressed through the crowd and received her healing as she touched the hem of Jesus' garment. We're told that Jesus felt that woman's touch, and turned, looking to see who had done it (Mk. 5:25-34). Now, Peter is the one diseased. He too has touched Jesus. But not in faith, as that woman had done. This is why the Lord shifts his standing—so the faithless, earnest disciple can find himself where the hemorrhaging woman of faith had been. In fact, even as he commands Peter to get behind him, Jesus moves so that Peter cannot fail to be where he should be! By turning away, Jesus not only prefigures the turn that needs to be made; he actually accomplishes it. And this is always the way of God's wrath. In spite of appearances, the divine judgment is always, always, always, at its heart, only ever mercy.

Yes, God turns his back on us. But never to put us in our place. Only ever to help us find it.

✝

When theologians say God is "simple" they mean that God does not have sides and so cannot be taken apart. With him, as Scripture says, there is "no variableness, neither shadow of turning" (Jam. 1:17).

We are decidedly *not* simple, of course. We're all of us thickets of contradictions, unmapped regions of unlikeness, uninterpreted messages in tongues. We are broken wheels within broken wheels. We not only do what we do not want to do, we do not even know much, if anything, about what we have done, or why we did it, or how. We're always standing in our own light, casting a chaos of crisscrossed shadows. But the good news is that God's simplicity can heal us, even if that healing is never quick, never easy.

Today's readings from Genesis and Romans refer us to the story of Abraham and Sarah. Genesis tells us that their names were changed. And today's Psalm identifies us as "of Jacob's line." His name was changed too. But not to the same effect. Jacob did receive a new name—*Israel*, the one who strives with God and Man and prevails. But this new name does not displace or eradicate the old one. Twice he is told by God—by God!—that he will no longer be called Jacob. But he is so called—even by God, and almost immediately.

The oddity of that fact is not lost on St Augustine, who found in it a mystical significance: "Jacob's grandfather Abraham's name was changed... And from that time he was not called Abram... But Jacob, after he had received another name, was called both Jacob and Israel."

Why is this? Augustine surmises it must be because the name "Abraham" refers to a calling to be fulfilled in this world, while "Israel" does not. Christians, he concludes, are in this present age always *both* Jacob *and* Israel: "Jacob in fact; Israel in hope." In the age to come, however, "Jacob" will be left behind.

Augustine's exegesis is lamentably bound up with supersessionism and anti-Jewishness. But he's nonetheless right to notice that in the Scriptures Israel continues to be called Jacob. And he's right to acknowledge the ongoing clash between fact and truth that marks the day-to-day experience of the faithful. He draws the wrong conclusion from these truths, however.

The Psalms again and again identify God as the God of Jacob. And when God reveals himself to Moses at the Burning Bush, he names himself the God of Abraham, Isaac, *and Jacob*. So, it is not that we shall cease to be Jacob when we have become Israel. The promise of salvation is one of *integration*: "When the Lord restores the fortunes of his people, Jacob will rejoice; Israel will be glad" (Ps. 14:7).

We are promised the marriage feast, not a great divorce.

Much of what we've learned and taught has suggested otherwise, I know. But when Jesus calls us to deny ourselves, he does not require anything that is in any way masochistic, destructive, or harmful.

Yes, those who want to save their life will lose it, and only those who lose their life for his sake, and for the sake of the gospel, will save it. But that "losing" is ours, a movement of love made possible by love, our freedom gracefully answering God's.

Nothing good is taken from us or kept from us. All that is lost in this "losing" is what we truly long to be free of—everything false, foul, vicious, cruel, diseased. The truth hurts, to be sure; but it never harms. In fact, it hurts only because it reveals how we have been harmed. God humbles, but never humiliates us, never desires our shame.

As we heal, we become more fully ourselves, not less. We increase as Christ increases in us. Self-control is the culminating fruit of the Spirit, after all (Gal. 5:23)! The mystery is, that increase, that growth comes only as we *decrease* as he did and does, growing down in humility, which is the very growth of God (Col. 2:19).

Near the end of his life, Fr Pedro Arrupe, S.J., the so-called Second Ignatius, suffered a debilitating stroke. As a young man, he had served as a missionary in Japan. He was in Hiroshima on the Feast of the Transfiguration, August 6th, 1945, when the atomic bomb exploded over the city. By the time he suffered the stroke in 1981, he had become a singularly controversial figure, renowned in some circles and despised in others for his work among refugees and his commitment to instituting the renewals and reforms called for by the Second Vatican Council. The stroke left him partially paralyzed. Soon, he couldn't speak at all and was restricted to the infirmary. He was forced to resign his post as Superior General of the Jesuit order, a post he had held for almost twenty years.

In act widely interpreted as a rebuke to Arrupe and an official reversal of his reforming project, as well as a shot across the bow of other religious orders, John Paul II suspended the ordinary governance of the Society and passed over the man Arrupe had selected to run the order in his absence. George Weigel, one of

John Paul II's biographer's, called the Pope's act an "intervention" and "shock therapy." Arrupe gave no public response. Two years after he had suffered the stroke, during the opening session of the Congregation that had been called to elect his successor, Arrupe was wheeled into the meeting room so he could read these words:

> More than ever I find myself in the hands of God. This is what I have wanted all my life from my youth. But now there is a difference: the initiative is entirely with God. It is indeed a profound spiritual experience to know and feel myself so totally in God's hands.

I tell Fr Arrupe's story to clear up what I mean when I say we are called to decrease, to grow down into God's humility. I do *not* mean that we need to be "cut down to size" by sickness or by our superiors. God does, indeed, "take us down," but never to break our spirit. God is ever graceful; he never resorts to disgracing us. He humbles us so we can be exalted with his exaltation.

Fr Arrupe, suffering indignity upon indignity, could rejoice in being in God's hands just because he knew whose hands they were. His sickness did not teach him that wisdom. He learned it in prayer, and in the presence of the poor, those left destitute of every help but God's.

✝

In Mark's Gospel, Peter, unbelievably, is the model disciple. Not because of anything he does, exactly. Just because Jesus continues to call him—in spite of whatever he has done or failed to do.

In the end, after Peter has taken Jesus aside and rebuked him; after he has spoken so stupidly on the mountain; after he has fallen asleep in the garden while Jesus begs for his support; after he has repeatedly denied knowing Jesus, even under oath, the women who find the empty tomb are told: "Go, tell the disciples *and Peter* that Jesus is already in Galilee; as he promised, he will meet you there" (Mk. 16:7).

Peter, wonderfully, shows up in Galilee, as do the women who at first fled in fear from the tomb and the angel's charge. He shows up as both Simon and Peter, both Jacob and Israel. Like Abraham, unlike Judas, he did not let his soul, as good as dead, or his failing faith, or his shame, drive him to despair. Instead, he put his body exactly where Jesus said it should be. He showed up—in spite of everything. So, his life shines with the transfiguring light of God.

This, then, is the gospel Mark proclaims: Jesus always speaks the last word, and that word is always a summons, a bidding, a welcome, a wooing. God always remembers our name—our *names*. Just so, we're never, never, never without hope.

In today's Epistle, Paul marvels that Abraham "did not weaken in faith when he considered his own body, which was already as good as dead... or when he considered the barrenness of Sarah's womb" (Rom. 4:19). But there is something even more marvelous— those who consider their *souls* without losing faith.

Lent is a time for numbering our sins. That is why the Lenten prayer of St Ephrem includes this petition: "Grant me to see my own transgressions, and not to judge my brother." But it is even more a time for remembering our identity as the Beloved.

Wonderfully, God has no sides. And that means we can come apart in his presence—without fear, without risk. God does not change. And that means we can be changed, reconciled not only to him and others, but also to ourselves.

This, finally, is the rock on which all things are founded: we are not what we fear we are; we are not who our enemies say we are; we are not what life has made of us; we are not what we have made of ourselves. No, we are who God, the God of Jacob, knows us to be, and has called us to be. And he never stops calling us—even when we've forgotten our own names.

4

Transfiguring Obedience

A Sermon for the Third Sunday in Lent
Exodus 20:1-17; Psalm 19; 1 Corinthians 1:18-25; John 2:13-22

On January 23rd, 404 A.D., St Augustine, then bishop of Hippo in Roman North Africa, delivered one of his longest, wittiest—and angriest—sermons. As was usual for him during this season of his life, he had come from Hippo to Carthage, a leading city of the Roman empire and the center of African Christianity, at the invitation of Aurelius, bishop of Carthage. Aurelius, a dear friend and the leading bishop in the province, had asked Augustine, who himself by this time had been a bishop for almost a decade, to give the sermon at one of the services dedicated to the celebration of the popular Spanish martyr, St Vincent of Saragossa. On the day of the feast, however, as Augustine began his prepared remarks, some in the swelling crowd demanded he move the pulpit closer to them, out from the apse and near to the altar in the center of the basilica. He refused, and after some rowdy back-and-forth, suddenly stepped down and walked away—without having delivered his sermon.

The next day, after Aurelius had spoken, Augustine began his remarks by accepting responsibility for "yesterday's disturbance." "I was as much to blame as you," he says, "and even more, because of my responsibility to you." That said, he moves quickly to insist that what he and Aurelius had asked, given the disruptions, had been anything but unreasonable:

> So the only thing we were asking was that those
> few people who were pressing on the altar

railings would have the goodness to move up to the spaces next to the place where we were speaking. Was that a very big thing to ask? But that's just what they refused to listen to, and the disturbance followed...

In those words, he seems to downplay the conflict. But almost immediately, he again lets loose a rebuke, speaking not about "them" but to "you":

I'll tell you, to put the fear of God into you, not to make you fall... Don't let disobedience seem to you just a slight sin. Certainly, I'll tell you straight out. It would have made not the slightest difference whether you listened from here or from there; that there was space enough near us for a crowd to fill, both I knew and you also knew. What did your opposition spring from, your refusal to come over here, but solely and simply from your obstinacy? ... If you don't obey in a slight matter, are you going to obey in a greater one? Haven't you read what the Lord said, "Whoever is faithful in a small matter is also faithful in a great one; and whoever is unfaithful in a small matter is also unfaithful in a great one"?

As he develops his apology—if that's in fact what it should be called—Augustine remarks, somewhat passive-aggressively, that it was not *his* idea to place the pulpit in the apse in the first place. And he makes it clear, impertinently, that only his "master," Aurelias, had either a reason or the right to be offended. He also explains, even more hilariously, that he did not ask for permission to come down from the pulpit because he believed he knew what had to be done and trusted instead in Aurelius' forgiveness.

Here he is again in his own words:

> Of course, if I had consulted him and he had forbidden me, I wouldn't have been able to do anything now but obey. I would have been obliged not come down. So, I preferred to ask his pardon afterward for coming down from the pulpit without consulting him or his

instructing me to, rather than not do what I thought should be done.

(Apparently, then, in North Africa, as now, in Middle America, it was better to beg forgiveness than to ask permission.)

Having "cleared the air," Augustine finally declares his intentions for this new day: he means to give the Carthaginians a lengthy talk—on *obedience*. Believe it or not.

Rhetorically, this forces him into a difficult spot, not only because of the previous day's drama, but also because of the ongoing trouble with the Donatists. As Paul Griffiths explains:

> Faced by a disobedient congregation in Carthage, and with the Donatist difficulties very much in mind, Augustine... must preach obedience, but must do it in such a way as to validate the disobedience of the martyrs; he must affirm the importance of obedience to the

state, but not in such a way as to call into question the subversive refusal of such obedience characteristic of both Catholic and Donatist martyrs; and he must distinguish the obedience he requires of his congregations from that required of theirs by Donatist bishops.

Even if you aren't familiar with the historical or theological details , you can easily imagine how hard it must have been for Augustine, under strained pastoral circumstances, to talk gracefully about obedience. You can imagine it so easily because the same is more or less always true, no matter who talks about it or where or when they do. Obedience is transfiguring; the call to obedience is a word of promise. But due to all the ugly things we've said about authority and submission, and all the foul things we've done to ourselves and others in the name of virtue, it has become hard, if not out-and-out impossible, to say anything truly life-giving about obedience. Somehow, we have to come to see obedience in an altogether different light.

✝

On April 9, 1968, a Pentecostal pastor, Calvin Bacon, ordained by the Assemblies of God, attended Martin Luther King Jr.'s funeral at the Ebenezer Baptist Church in Atlanta. In July, Bacon's reflections were published in his denomination's magazine, *The Pentecostal Evangel*. In those reflections, Bacon admits that "the American Negroes had not been treated right." But he does not hesitate to condemn King's methods of resistance:

> I can't say I fully agreed with his "nonviolent civil disobedience." Nonviolence, yes. But I wasn't sure our definitions were the same. Civil disobedience, no: I knew the Scriptures state that we were to submit to our rulers.

Bacon remembers asking himself a series of questions at the end of the service: "Why all the trouble? How long will such violence last? Who is responsible? What is the solution?" And he also recalls that a passage from Scripture occurred to him on his drive home, a passage about obedience: "Let as many servants as are under the yoke count their own masters worthy of all honor, that the name of God and his doctrine be not blasphemed" (1 Tim. 6:1).

You heard me right: leaving Martin Luther King Jr.'s funeral—*Martin Luther King's!*—the passage that came to his preaching mind was one that requires slaves—*slaves!*—to stay in their place, submitting to their masters' God-ordained will. To do otherwise is tantamount to blasphemy.

In the light of that "revelation," Bacon reached an immediate conclusion; one many of his neighbors and colleagues must have shared: "Civil rights legislation and government spending cannot, I believe, meet the basic needs of the ghettos, but the gospel can."

He concludes that good white Christians must find some way "to help our black neighbors spiritually— through gospel preaching and Bible teaching"—as opposed to preaching "social revolution," as "their ministers" do.

That's shocking to hear, I know. But should it be?

Bacon can say what he says because of widespread convictions about authority and submission, superiority and obedience, convictions which, to put it sharply, align not with the law of Christ but with the spirit of Jim Crow. If we're honest, don't we have to admit that we, like him, have been shaped and misshaped by forms of Christianity deeply compromised by what Kosuke Koyama calls "the crusading mind"? Don't we have to admit that we, too, have been hoodwinked (!) by half-Christian myths that keep us accepting the status quo? There was a time, as Frederick Douglass said, that the sound of the slave-selling bell and the sound of the church-going bell were indistinguishable. The sound of shackles and whips mixed with the sound of hymns and praise. Have we un-rung those bells?

On January 6th, 2021—for Western Christians, the Feast of the Epiphany(!)—a mob stormed the Capitol in Washington, disrupting the process formalizing President Biden's election. Ironically, as I'm sure you remember, the insurrectionists presented themselves as patriots—many of them as *Christian* patriots—even as they mounted their attack on democratic principles and the symbolic center of their own government, some threatening death to their enemies. Even more bizarrely, in the days that followed a number of believers, including a few well-known figures, used the story of the temple cleansing, which we heard today in the Gospel reading, to justify the insurrection.

Obviously, even to mention these events is to invite controversy and to risk dismissal. But we have to face the ugly truths of our situation, truths that the storming of the Capital and the Christian defenses of it bring into painfully sharp relief. In Russell Moore's words, written for *Christianity Today* one year after the uprising, the capital attack "signaled a post-Christian church, not merely a post-Christian culture."

The situation is worse even than Moore allows.

During his time in the US, Bonhoeffer concluded that the prevailing American Protestantism was a

Christianity without Reformation—theologically unmoored and spiritually disoriented. Sadly, what he said then of the preaching he had heard in New York's mainline Protestant churches is effectively true of what can be heard now in so-called Bible-believing churches across the U.S.:

> The sermon has been reduced to parenthetical church remarks about newspaper events... [T]hey preach about virtually everything, only one thing is not addressed, or is addressed so rarely that I have as yet been unable to hear it, namely, the gospel of Jesus Christ, the cross, sin and forgiveness, death and life... [This Christianity is] an ethical and social idealism borne by a faith in progress that—who knows how—claims the right to call itself "Christian." And in the place of the church as the congregation of believers in Christ there stands the church as a social corporation.

I don't think it's at all a reactionary exaggeration to say that American Christianity—again, in its dominant forms—is and has been from the first impossibly conflicted and confused. Indeed, the reason these forms came to be dominant in the first place is that they agreed to serve the status quo, accepting, if not outright championing, what Martin Luther King Jr called "the giant triplets of racism, extreme materialism, and militarism," as well as sexism, ableism, and xenophobia (including anti-Catholicism and anti-Jewishness).

Hard as it is for us to accept, and loath as we may be to deal with what that acceptance would mean for us, the truth is that our agreement with the status quo could not have happened if we had remained true to the Gospel's promise and to our call as prophets of a future not our own.

Allow me, for a moment, to speak sharply. Pray for me as I do. For centuries, American Christians in positions of power have as a rule used God's name to excuse or warrant evils, endorsing corrupt ideals and validating oppressive systems. Explicitly or implicitly, intentionally or unconsciously, our foremost churches and ministries have customarily given themselves to what in effect is an ideological laundering operation for the powers that be, cleaning up demonic lies and satanic half-truths by mixing them with or hiding them under biblical proof texts and the language of traditional Christian doctrine.

Thus, Hosea's prophecy against Israel, spoken just before the fall of the Northern Kingdom, rings true for us, here and now:

> Hear the word of the LORD, ye children of Israel: for the LORD hath a controversy with the inhabitants of the land, because there is no truth, nor mercy, nor knowledge of God in the land. By swearing, and lying, and killing, and stealing, and committing adultery, they break out, and blood toucheth blood. (Hos. 4:1-2).

No doubt many of Hosea's contemporaries dismissed what he said as alarmist. Others, I'd guess, agreed much too quickly with what they thought he had said, sure they knew what he really meant, confident he was on their side. But this holds true, regardless: nothing and no-one but God can save us, and that salvation begins only in heart-shattering repentance and the once-for-all repudiation of all other gods.

If, then, we want to be free of the lies that blind us and the half-truths that make those lies believable, we must beg the Spirit to bring the whole truth of our situation to light—and come ourselves fully into that light, knowing that that means most of what we've said and done will be consumed in the Refiner's fire.

There is a certain kind of wisdom in these dominant, dominating forms of Christianity and the social orders they secure, without a doubt. The Apostle Paul calls it "the wisdom of this world." The wisdom exposed as cruelty by the grandeur of God shining on the battered face of a certain trouble-making prophet from Galilee. The wisdom we have to forsake, becoming fools with Christ and in him, so that we might receive the wisdom of God.

So, if we hope to return to God, if we hope to turn away from all the false gods we've made for ourselves, if we hope to be healed, if we hope to be healing presences, then we must "dwell under his shadow" (Hos. 14:7), the shadow cast by his mutilated body, suspended in godforsakeness.

Only the spat-upon God can help.

✝

In 1934, near the end of his time as a pastor in London, and only a few years after his time at Union Seminary in New York, Bonhoeffer gave a sermon (in English) on 2 Corinthians 12:9 and St Paul's theology of the cross—strength made perfect in weakness.

In his opening lines, he urged the congregation to be honest with themselves. Can they admit that what the Gospel says about weakness is impossible to square with the worldly, aristocratic conceptions of strength they hold dear? Are they ready to deal with what that conflict means for them, for their lives?

> It was the attitude towards the problem of
> weakness in the world which made everybody

followers or enemies of Christianity. Against the new meaning which Christianity gave to the weak, against this glorification of weakness, there has always been the strong and indignant protest of an aristocratic philosophy of life which glorified strength and power and violence as the ultimate ideals of humanity. We have observed this very fight going on up to our present day.

He insists that because "God suffered on the cross," suffering and those who suffer are holy, and the strong must always look up to the weak. Then, he draws this conclusion:

> Christianity stands or falls by its revolutionary protest against violence, arbitrariness and pride of power, and by its apologia for the weak. I feel that Christianity is doing too little in making these points rather than doing too much. Christianity has adjusted itself much too easily to the worship of power. It should give much more offence, more shock to the world,

than it is doing. Christianity should take a much more definite stand for the weak than for the potential moral right of the strong... Our God is a suffering God. Suffering conforms humanity to God. The suffering person is in the likeness of God. "My strength is made perfect in weakness" says God. Wherever one of us, in physical or social or moral or religious weakness, is aware of our existence and likeness to God, there we are sharing God's life, there we feel God being with us, there we are open for God's strength, that is God's grace, God's love, God's comfort, which passeth all understanding and all human values. God is glorified in the weak as God in Christ was glorified on the cross. God is mighty where humanity is nothing.

It can't be any easier for us to hear this now than it was for them to hear it then. But it is no less vital.

In his sermon to the Carthaginians, preached 1500 years earlier than Bonhoeffer's, Augustine cleverly appeals to Jesus' example. He tells his hearers they are not expected to "kindle the sun, make the moon run its monthly course of waning and waxing, cause the stars to shine from the sky..." or to "... open the eyes of the blind, crack open the ears of the deaf, drive off the fevers of the sick, raise up the flesh of the dead." They *are,* however, expected in these matters to obey their bishops, because in this way they obey the will of God the bishops have made known.

Jesus obeyed the Father as his equal. But he also obeyed his mother. And while many bristle at being called a slave, Jesus gladly took that title for himself. He made himself not only the slave of the Father and the slave of his mother but also the slave of all—"including," he says, "even you."

Augustine mischievously parries an anticipated objection:

> Somebody will say, "My bishop should follow my Lord's example, and serve me as my slave." I'm telling your graces—let those get the point

who can—if he wasn't serving you as your slave, he wouldn't be giving you orders.

Then, in the closing lines of his sermon, which he admits has taken far too long, Augustine reminds his hearers how Christ, as the disciples' slave, commanded them to fetch from the nearest village the foal providentially kept for them.

His reading of the story illustrates what he takes to be the very essence of Christian obedience:

> What is this foal, tied up in the village over against them, on which nobody had ever sat, what can it be, but the people of the nations tied up in the devil's chains, and nobody had ever sat on it because it had never carried any prophet? It's untied; it's fetched; it carries God; it's ridden by the Lord; it's directed by the Lord along the way; it's admonished by the Lord with a whip. Both by those who complied and fetched the foal was obedience displayed, and by those who let the foal go the moment they

heard the Lord needed it... Which are you, my brothers and sisters? Which do you want to be: the ones untying the foal, or the foal? You dare not claim for yourselves the role of those the foal was united by; it was the apostles who did this. This is the role of men in charge, the role we ourselves have to sustain with whatever strength the Lord is pleased to grant us—with total, anxious vigilance; it's in this role that I am speaking to you. You are the foal. Be obedient to those who are leading you off to carry the Lord. Of course, my dearest friends, you must reflect on the manner in which the disciples untied the foal and led it along to the Lord. They were leading it, and it was following them; I mean, they weren't dragging it, while it was digging in its heels. And yet, because we are talking about our service, our being your slaves, when the disciples were leading the foal to the Lord, they were really, in fact, being the slaves of the foal. That's how we too act as your slaves, when we lead you to the Lord, when we teach you obedience and admonish you. If your weakness wasn't being served in this way, you wouldn't have come to listen to us today.

Augustine's playfulness lightens the burden, or at least shifts the weight. But it does not quite set us free.

He is right, of course, to say that God's mastery is to our good. And he is right to say that Jesus, as God living the human life, acted both as master and as slave, first and last. But he seems unable, or unwilling, to accept how Jesus' enactment irrevocably revolutionized these roles.

Whatever is right about it, then, Augustine's reading of the story of the Triumphal Entry leaves the impression that Christ's readiness to take on the form of a slave in effect assures the appropriateness of slavery as an institution. But it comes nearer the truth, I believe, to say Jesus took the form of a slave not only to dignify humility and service, but also to overcome mastery and domination and to heal the humiliations they inflict, revealing once-for-all how inhumane it is for one human to own another, and how blasphemous it is to regard others as in any sense inferior or unworthy. Christ in his life and death does not secure our social orders or our systems of authority: he calls them into question, exposing their pretentions as absurd, delivering us from their showy claims on our allegiance. And he calls us to embody an altogether different obedience, which he ordained and enacted, the obedience not of servility or coercion, but the obedience of perfect mutuality and shared flourishing, covenantal reciprocity and common delight.

Needless to say, Augustine was not alone in his mistake. To this day, we continue by and large to ignore the fuller implications of the Gospel, to resist the fulfillment of Jesus' Spirit-baptized project. Far too often, we, no less than the Catholics in ancient Carthage or the white Pentecostals in Jim Crow Atlanta, insist on obedience only insofar as it fixes our way of life, guaranteeing our security against those whom we fear or our superiority over those whom we despise. Our sins are no different from our forefathers'.

Nevertheless, the Spirit continues to call us to repentance, wooing us back toward the obedience that Christ accomplished for us, the way of life that frees us for freedom, releasing us from the pressures of the status quo, and empowering us to intercede for and to intervene on behalf of those who're being crushed or pushed aside by the way the world works.

Augustine was not wrong to call the Carthaginians to obey their bishops. Our obedience to God necessarily takes the shape of submission to human authorities, not only in our churches and our families, but also in our societies. And he was not wrong to warn them about the dangers of disobedience. But if we leave it there, we have done nothing—or at least not enough—to contradict the line of thinking that led some to condemn MLK's civil disobedience as unscriptural and allowed others to use the story of the cleansing of the temple as justification for sedition and violence.

We need to catch the spirit of Augustine's sermon, the playfulness of it. We need to be careful not to take ourselves too seriously, especially when we're lecturing others about obedience, and even more especially when we're lecturing them about obeying us! But we also need to say something he did not: our obedience is good only if it is a share in God's, because only God's obedience frees us for loving as we have been loved.

In the opening meditation in his Large Catechism, Robert Jenson insists God's laws are not alien or onerous for us, but vital and revitalizing. Make no mistake, he says, God does intend for us to be "faithful rather than questing, pious rather than neglectful, communal rather than autonomously individual, chaste rather than liberated, helpful to the fabric of community rather than harmful to it, mutually pleasured rather than covetous." But we must not think this intention is imposed on us against our desire or to our harm. On the contrary, they constitute our good.

This is the wonder of God's infinite, generative humility: our obedience, whenever it is true, turns out to be nothing less than a sharing in his sovereignty, a participation in the everlasting dominion by which all things are called into being and drawn into perfection. So, whatever else we say, we have to say this clearly: our obedience neither pleases God nor appeases him; it does not earn his favor. No, God requires our obedience because only in submission to God's will can we be awakened to the reality of our neighbors' joys and sorrows.

When we obey, therefore, we find that our obedience is itself a gift, a favor from God, a joy that draws us up into God's transfiguring delight in us, assuring us of his devotion to us. And this, in the end, is why Christ obeyed, and took the time to learn how to obey—so that he might create for us a way to become for others what he is for us and for God.

Today's Psalm expresses exactly this truth: "The law of the Lord is perfect and revives the soul... The statutes of the Lord are just and rejoice the heart" (Ps. 19:7-8).

Do you see what that means? When God's will is most perfectly done, we are most fully ourselves. So, Herbert prays:

> O let thy sacred will
>   All thy delight in me fulfill!
> Let me not think an action mine own way
>   But as thy love shall sway,
> Resigning up the rudder to thy skill.

If we live like *that,* resigned to God's sacred skill, we will be truly free (not autonomous!)—liberated liberators, suffering as God suffers. Just so, only so, can we rightly protest against the world's violences and give that "shock" that unrings bells.

The unringing *is* possible. As Sister Rosetta Tharpe taught us, there are strange things happening every day.

> There are strange things happening everyday
> If you want to view the climb
> You must learn to quit your lyin'

74

There are strange things happening everyday
If you heal right through the lies
You can live right all the ties
There are strange things happening everyday

Healing right through the lies. Living right all the ties. *This* is the Spirit's Lenten work. *This* is "entire sanctification."

We won't be able to live the strange way of life set aside for us if we can't believe that God in fact sees us as friends, as partners, as co-regents. Paul told the Corinthians that he and his ministry team had no interest in dominating them, in lording over their faith. We want, he said, to be " helpers for your joy" (2 Cor. 1:24). He could say that because he knew that's how Christ related to him.

We are God's glory, and God is ours. As St Maximus says, divinity and humanity are paradigms of each other. God is the lifter of our heads; the last thing he wants us is for us to grovel. What he wants us is for us to be his equals—loving as he loves, knowing as he knows. We are, remember, flesh of his flesh and bone of his bone.

Origen said it again and again: Jesus is Lord of lords, not a master of slaves; King of kings, not a sovereign over subjects; a High Priest among high priests, not a hierarch among acolytes.

Christ calls you into obedience, then, not to impose his or his Father's will on you, not to coerce you into conformity with some moral standard; not to test the sincerity of your devotion; not to exploit your gifts; not to prove to you your frailty; not to rub your nose in your failures.

No, he calls you into obedience so you can hear the voice he heard in the bowels of the Jordan, and again on the peak of Tabor, and know that what is said is said of *you*.

This, no doubt, seems too good to be true. That's how you know it must be.

5

Transfiguring
Doubt

A Sermon for the Fourth Sunday in Lent
Numbers 21:4-9; Psalm 107:1-3, 17-22; Ephesians 2:1-10; John 3:14-21

Today, we catch Jesus mid-sentence. He's responding to a Pharisee, "a leader of the Jews," who has sought him out, deep in the night, for questioning.

We're accustomed to regarding Pharisees as supervillains, of course. But John singles out this particular Pharisee, Nicodemus, requiring us to see his face and to hear his voice.

As we listen to his exchange with Jesus, an exchange which is at times painfully awkward, it becomes harder and harder to deny that his disbelief and misunderstandings make more sense to us than Jesus' dark wisdom does. Nicodemus seems earnest and goodhearted, if also out of his depth. Square, perhaps, but not in the least sanctimonious or hypocritical.

Prejudices die hard, however. When we're told he came "by night" (Jn 3:2), but not *why*, we're quick to infer the worst. Augustine says Nicodemus "wished to be enlightened and feared to be known." Calvin suggests, rather harshly, that "his timidity was excessive; for his eyes were dazzled, as it were, by the splendor of his own greatness and reputation." But we need not assume Nicodemus was fainthearted or self-important. Perhaps he came at night in order to protect Jesus. Or perhaps he came at night on the spur of the moment, suddenly, because he was exhausted with holding in his admiration for Jesus. Or perhaps it was not so much admiration as dread that drove him to Jesus.

Regardless, he came. He made his confession. He asked his questions. He listened to Jesus' response. He carried that response away with him, let it grow in his soul's depths. In this way, more or less in spite of himself, Nicodemus, the Pharisee of Pharisees, models for us the way of faith—a way that is always stranger than we could've imagined we would want.

Nicodemus first comes to Jesus with a confession: "Rabbi, we know that you are a teacher who has come from God; for no one can do these signs that you do apart from the presence of God" (Jn 3:2). He moves toward God with what he knows. He soon discovers, however—almost immediately, in fact—that there is much he does not know, and that he understands little, if anything, about what he does know.

Yes, Jesus is a teacher. Yes, he is from God. Nicodemus' words are true. But they are true in ways he cannot yet grasp.

This is why Jesus answers Nicodemus' questions as he does, forcing a necessary confusion. As with him, so with us: "discipleship" names a process of continual unlearning, a movement into instructed, instructive ignorance. Thus, Nicodemus' perplexity serves as a warning to us, and a promise—reminding us that no matter who we are or what we've accomplished, the truth in its fullness is too lively for us. Grace cannot save us without first losing us, which means grace always makes things awkward.

Lent is a good time to remember that Jesus was anything but a simple teacher. In the Gospels, his teachings are met almost always either with incredulity and confusion or fury and fear. His hearers are usually left astonished or incensed. In fact, in John's Gospel, virtually everyone misunderstands everything Jesus says and does. Nicodemus' astonishment, then, is anything but unusual. In the opening of Luke's Gospel, the angel Gabriel appears out of the blue to the priest

Zechariah, declaring a longed-for word of promise: "Do not be afraid, Zechariah, for your prayer has been heard. Your wife Elizabeth will bear you a son, and you will name him John. You will have joy and gladness, and many will rejoice at his birth" (Lk 1:13-14). Zechariah responds with a weirdly managerial or philosophical question: "How will I know that this is so? For I am an old man, and my wife is getting on in years?" Gabriel's response is quick and sharp: "Because you did not believe my words, which will be fulfilled in their time, you will become mute, unable to speak, until the day these things occur" (Lk 1:20).

Afterward, Gabriel appears to Mary, bearing and delivering another promise: "Do not be afraid, Mary, for you have found favor with God. And now, you will conceive in your womb and bear a son, and you will name him Jesus" (Lk. 1:30-31). She responds with a faithful question: "How can this be, since I am a virgin?" (Lk. 1:24). As Paul Griffiths has said,

> Zechariah's question is skeptical and individualistic—"How can I know this is true?"—

while Mary's question is trusting and personal: "How can this be, since I am a virgin?" These two questions provide a kind of a rubric, laying out for us the essential difference between faithless and faithful questions.

Earlier in John's Gospel, "the Jews'" (a cadre of Judean authorities, it seems) had asked a question much like Zechariah's: "You think you can raise up this temple in three days?" (Jn 2:20). And Nicodemus' first question seems to be of a similar kind. "How can anyone be born after having grown old? Can one enter a second time into the mother's womb and be born?" (Jn 3:4). This question betrays incredulity, for sure. It's not dismissive, necessarily, and not accusatory; but it is at least somewhat skeptical. His second question, however, seems to be the same as Mary's: "How can these things be? (Jn 3:9).

By drawing our attention to the shift between Nicodemus' first question and his second, John shows us what it means to move away from bad certainties and what is falsely called knowledge toward the truth.

He admits his doubts and lets himself ask the stupid questions that are rising up in his heart because his faith, weak as it is, seeks understanding.

Not all questions are faithless. Sometimes, in fact, the only faithful response to truth is a question that owns our confusions. That kind of doubt, George MacDonald's assures us, is the hammer that shatters the windows obscured by "human fancies" and lets in the pure light.

In one of his "unspoken sermons," MacDonald praises Job's desire to know God honestly, a desire he sees expressed in Job's voiced doubts:

> Doubts are the messengers of the Living One to rouse the honest. They are the first knock at our door of things that are not yet, but have to be, understood; and theirs in general is the inhospitable reception of angels that do not come in their own likeness. Doubt must precede every deeper assurance; for uncertainties are what we first see when we look

into a region hitherto unknown, unexplored, unannexed.

Lent is a season of transfiguration in part because it makes room for us to be confused, allowing us not only to admit our ignorance, but also to appreciate it as a movement toward understanding—or at least toward the kind of *mis*understanding that God can use to our good. During Lent, we learn to entertain those awkward angels, those graceful messages, that come in the likeness of our enemies.

✝

It's hard to talk about doubt without slipping into cliché or, worse, into sentimentality. Some of us, God knows why, talk glibly about it—as if doubt were sexy. Others of us, even less sensibly, talk as if doubt were foreign to the truly Christian life. If we're honest, however, we'll have to admit that much of what passes for doubt is nothing but honest hesitation, the inevitable upshot of generations of poor or bad teaching, teaching which trades in simplicities and cheap certainties, often eschewing pain at all costs, leaving us to feel that our salvation depends not on the mystery of faith, sustained by God's devotion to us, but on our own grasp of our own beliefs or on the intensity of our desire for religious experiences.

It seems that we're becoming less and less patient with the work of learning the truth, more and more afraid of whatever we do not already understand, all too easily angered by anything that demands serious attention or care. As a rule, we can hardly deal with the challenge of honest questions, much less the anguish and turmoil that come in authentic "dark night" experiences of doubt and crises of faith. Nicodemus, then, seems to us like a fool, not a saint. And we laugh at his questions without bothering to listen to them.

In *Night of the Confessor*, Tomáš Halík argues that "simple faith" cannot endure the harshness of reality for long. Sooner or later, he says, we're thrown into crisis because of the "the multivalence of life." Eventually, inevitably, "the profound ambivalence of reality" shatters the insipid, fatuous systems of control

we've made for ourselves and others — including those
we've made in God's name. Our fundamentalisms and
fanaticisms, made and kept by violence, are no match
for reality. So, Halík warns, we have to be saved from
"simple faith."

But not so we might have "great faith." That, too,
always proves false. According to Halík what we need is
neither simple nor great faith but instead *the faith of
God,* which is what is left of our faith after it has died
and been raised to life, after it has been purged by the
Spirit:

> The faith that undergoes the fire of the cross
> without retreating probably loses much of what
> it tended to be identified with or what it was
> itself accustomed to, even though it was merely
> superficial. Much will be scorched away.
> However, its new maturity will be chiefly
> evident from the fact that it will no longer
> appear "in armor": instead it will be a bit like
> that "naked faith" that the mystics speak of. It
> will not be aggressive or arrogant, let alone

impatient in its relationship with others. Yes, compared to "great" and "firm" faith it may appear small and insignificant—it will be like nothing, like a mustard seed.

We should pray continually to be delivered from childish simplicities and illusions of greatness into the childlike seriousness and unaffectedness of our all-too-human God. The cry for that purification is at the heart of all Lenten spirituality.

✝

Today's Gospel, as I said, catches Jesus mid-sentence. The first thing we hear him say is this: "And just as Moses lifted up the serpent in the wilderness, so must the Son of Man be lifted up, that whoever believes in him may have eternal life" (Jn 3:14-15).

Gregory Nazianzen, in one of his Easter sermons, argues that the serpent was a type not of Christ but of *death*, which Christ by his dying and being dead destroyed. It's hard to overstate the power of this passage:

> That brazen serpent was hung up as a remedy
> for the biting serpents, not as a type of him who
> suffered for us, but as a contrast; and it saved
> those who looked upon it, not because they
> believed it to live, but because it was killed, and
> killed with it the powers that were subject to it,
> being destroyed as it deserved.

Augustine, in a homily on the passage, takes a different tack, at fist, arguing that the biting sermons are "sins, from the mortality of the flesh." The serpent, he says, is the Lord's death: "For as death came by the serpent, it was figured by the image of a serpent." Then he runs through a series of contrasts:

> The serpent's bite was deadly, the Lord's death
> is life-giving. A serpent is gazed on that the
> serpent may have no power. What is this? A
> death is gazed on, that death may have no
> power. But whose death? The death of life: if it
> may be said, the death of life...

Augustine revels in the paradoxes and reversals:

> Shall I hesitate to utter that which the Lord has deigned to do for me? Is not Christ the life? And yet Christ hung on the cross. Is not Christ life? And yet Christ was dead. But in Christ's death, death died. Life dead slew death; the fullness of life swallowed up death; death was absorbed in the body of Christ.

Following their lead, we may say, then, that Jesus is not only like the brazen serpent, lifted up in death so that death might be brought low; he is also like the *biting* serpents, striking us so we come alive, wounding us for healing.

The truth hurts, we say. And so it does. But it never *harms*. So it is with Jesus, who is the Truth. He, our Good Physician, only ever heals. But healing is often painful. So, when needed, he wisely troubles us toward the change we need to make. He is the very God whom Scripture says curses and blesses, hurts and heals, kills and makes alive (Deut. 32:39). And not for no reason the saints, including Augustine, speak of the wounding arrows of love. "Faithful are the wounds of a friend" (Prov. 27:6), the Scripture says. And no one is a better friend to us than God.

We should not be surprised, then, that there is a *bite* in Jesus' question to Nicodemus: "Are you a teacher of Israel, and yet you do not understand these things?" (Jn 3:10). Or that there is a bite in his answer to Nicodemus' questions: "What is born of the flesh is flesh, and what is born of the Spirit is spirit" (Jn 3:6).

Jesus is kind, always; but he does not play nice. He is too good a friend to belittle us with politeness. "A bruised reed shall he not break, and smocking flax shall he not quench." But recall if you can the rest of that promise: he does indeed "send forth judgment unto victory" (Mt. 12:20). That is why his name can be trusted (Mt 12:21).

Nicodemus, remember, came to Jesus with a confession: "Rabbi, we know that you are a teacher who has come from God" (Jn 3:2). He leaves with nothing but the awareness that he knows nothing. That awareness, however, was everything he needed for the time being.

✝

The Gospel does not tell us how Jesus' conversation with Nicodemus ends or what Nicodemus made of it. He drops from the story. But then he reappears at the end, and raises another question, this time in Jesus' defense: "Our law does not judge people without first giving them a hearing to find out what they are doing, does it?" (Jn 7:51).

Other Pharisees rebuke Nicodemus for his trouble: "Surely you're not also from Galilee, are you?" (Jn 7:52). Their question is, of course, an accusation. One that betrays their prejudices. But it also hides the seeds of a truth. What Nicodemus does next shows those seeds have germinated; he appears at Jesus' tomb:

> After these things, Joseph of Arimathea, who was a disciple of Jesus, though a secret one

because of his fear of the Jews, asked Pilate to let him take away the body of Jesus. Pilate gave him permission; so he came and removed his body. Nicodemus, who had at first come to Jesus by night, also came, bringing a mixture of myrrh and aloes, weighing about a hundred pounds. They took the body of Jesus and wrapped it with the spices in linen cloths, according to the burial custom of the Jews. (Jn 19:38-40)

Tradition holds that Nicodemus later became a believer, expelled from the Sanhedrin and exiled from Jerusalem. But he obviously did not come to believe the night of his encounter— at least not in any sense he could have recognized. And even here, at the end of the Gospel, as he comes to anoint the dead body of Jesus, he is not named a believer—not even a secret one (as Joseph of Arimathea is). Still, John wants us to see Nicodemus and to remember how he came to be here, kneeling in tears beside this dead body. He wants us to know that we too can be "from Galilee." The very place out of which no prophet arises becomes the site of our marriage to the one whose words are life.

By the way it tells Nicodemus' odd conversion story, John's Gospel maps for us the way into the truth that is the life of the words of God: first, our bad confessions, made honestly, lead to questions; then those questions, taken seriously, lead to doubt; and doubt, at long last, leads to tearful *silence*—the purifying anguish made possible by the death of God. At last, left with nothing but God's faith, we find we can see the truth our confession had kept from us at first and then for us.

✝

In today's Epistle, we hear that we are saved by grace through faith, not by anything we've done but as the gift of God, a gift that comes with no strings attached. "For we are what he has made us, created in Christ Jesus for good works, which God prepared beforehand to be our way of life" (Eph. 2:9-10).

Paul's words force a question: If we are indeed what he makes us, then who was Nicodemus? How was he created? What works had been made for him to do? And the answer comes: Nicodemus is a teacher—not only from Israel, but *of* Israel.

Do you see it? Can you hear it? Jesus' biting question, "Are you a teacher of Israel?," which we had taken at first to be derisive and belittling, proves at last to be the very word that creates Nicodemus' calling and empowers him to fulfill it. He flowers into his fulness.

God wounds, to be sure. But God's wounds *heal.* This is why Fr Jean Pierre de Caussade could assure a postulant who'd written to him about the darkness of her doubts that she had nothing to fear.

> Your state, although, in truth, very crucifying, is
> nevertheless, and indeed on that account, very
> safe, very purifying and very sanctifying. You
> need fear no danger, as long as you hold by
> Fénélon's great rule: despair entirely of
> yourself, and put not an atom of confidence in

anything but God alone, who, from the very
stones can raise up children to Abraham.

Struggling with Jesus at night, as Jacob, his father, had
done, Nicodemus teaches us how to be an Israel—one
who strives with God and Man and prevails, not in
strength but in weakness; not through knowledge, but
through learned ignorance; not by certainty, but by
doubt.

Yes, the crucified God is dangerous. He is a biting
serpent. But all he kills is what endangers us. God is the
destroyer of all that destroys, the death of death, the
negation of all that keeps us from ourselves and one
another. Thus, when all is said and done, our doubts
turn out to be nothing—the nothing from which God
creates our faith.

6

Transfiguring Repentance

A Sermon for the Fifth Sunday in Lent
Jeremiah 31:31-34; Psalm 51:1-13; Hebrews 5:5-10; John 12:20-33

I am not sure how to begin. I need to talk about repentance, which, of course, in turn requires me to talk about *sin*. But that puts me in a bind because I'm convinced that our—*my*—sense of what counts as sin, and what should be done about it, is seriously warped and almost entirely untrustworthy.

In an earlier draft of this sermon, I said that nothing is more sinful than what we've said about sin and what we've done in the name of our hatred for sin. I stand by that claim. But on its own, as I had written it, it was too straightforward, I think. It suggested I'm not as confused as you are, or at least that you and I are more enlightened than "they" are. It's hard, perhaps even impossible, to talk about sin without sinning.

We're all familiar with the traditional language of sin and repentance, faith and forgiveness. We all know we're supposed to confess our sins and give thanks to God for his mercy. "There but for the grace of God go I," we say. But what if our familiarity works against us? What if the ways we're using the language we've received keeps us from discerning what is truly wrong in and between us?

Over the years, I've found that what I learned to think (and to feel, and to do) about sin tended to be somehow self-absorbed and self-negating, naïve and grandiose, individualist and sectarian both-at-once. Reflecting on that strange reality, I wrote these lines in that earlier draft of this sermon I mentioned:

We've cared more about appearances than reality, straining at gnats while swallowing camels, obsessing about trivialities while neglecting the weightier matters of the law. In direct contradiction to the wisdom of Scripture, we take part in and benefit from systems that favor the powerful, overlooking or even excusing their abuses. We allow violence after violence to be done in our name and God's. We're nice, but not kind; indulgent, not compassionate; precautious, not tactful; careless, not openhearted; permissive, not forgiving. Instead of hopeful and forbearing, we've been punitive and exacting, demanding what God has not required. And instead of feeling real alarm about these sins, and instead of committing ourselves to making right what our wrongs have done, we've recoiled in contempt from our neighbors or lashed out at ourselves in disgust—as if God were pleased by our shame and self-loathing.

Now, I'm pretty sure all that's not entirely fair. As soon as I'd finished writing it, it struck me more as fiery accusation than illuminating description. But be that as it may, I know this—I don't know myself well enough to repent as I should. The heart cannot know itself in that way. But there is hope, nonetheless, because God, our God, tries the heart, seeking out its secrets. He has shown us who he is; so, we can trust him. We can rest in knowledge that he can save us from our sins, even the sin of false repentance.

✝

We're not made to sin. Today's Psalm, Psalm 51, reminds us of that. Doing wrong is bad for us. It pales our humanity, strips us of our dignity. We, like Paul in Romans 7, find we can't *not* do it. But we nonetheless hate having done it.

The *Miserere* also shows us that there is an even lower layer: we sin because we have been sinned against. "Behold, I was shapen in iniquity; and in sin did my mother conceive me" (Ps. 51:5). We are marked, all of us, by what others have done and left undone. We have not because we ask not, James tell us. We have not because we ask amiss. But more needs to be said: we have not in part because we have not known what to ask, because others have failed to ask for us. We often ask amiss because no one has taught us how to pray as we ought—or how to forgive, or how to celebrate, or how to show thanks.

We don't take nearly seriously enough the reality of our interdependence, the interwovenness of our shared being. And for that reason, it's impossible for us to make sense of the guilt and shame we together actually bear.

The truth is, we suffer the weight not only of our own guilt but also the guilt of fathers and mothers, the guilt of our ancestors, first to last. We bear the weight of the long history of violence through which our species has evolved. Who knows how these evils, and the damage done by them, have misshaped our consciousness, disfigured our perception?

Evil has wounded us, as it has wounded all things, at the source, the very heart of our existence. We do not exist as we should—in full, unstinted flourishing. We exist largely in fragments and remains, mostly estranged from ourselves and others. Our depravity arises from the fact that we are often deprived of the care we actually need from others, the care we deserve. But they too are deprived. And so are the ones who damaged them.

So, we're caught in a trap we cannot escape, sick with a sickness for which there is no cure. This is what it means to be "fallen."

As the Orthodox theologian, Olivier Clément, explains in his remarkable book *On Human Being*:

> From our own experience and from our observation of others we are aware that human nature is damaged. Damaged, first of all, within each one of us: the "self" is a shadow theater of neurotic characters, and it is they who are pulling our strings instead of the other way

about. Our faculties are disunited and out of order. While the rational intelligence is busy making distinctions, the "heart," in obedience to dark subconscious forces, is obliterating them. We are turned this way and that, lacking any center of balance. Not only are we disunited as individuals, we are the same in relation to each other. Whether we are alone or involved with others, we remain separate and hostile, alone even in our involvement.

That brings me back to the point. We cannot save ourselves from this trouble. We need God to deliver us. Not to overlook our sins, but to see us in our plight and to see to our rescue, our healing. Not to absolve us, merely, but to *heal* us—altering our inner condition so that we can begin to cooperate with him and one another, making restitution for our wrongs.

We need God to be generous, not permissive; kind, not nice; annihilating everything false in us, anything corrupt or diseased. We need God to create cleanness in us, obliterating all separateness, venality, and hostility, and enlivening us with the clarity of his own life so that we can live as we long to live, as we are meant to liv—in mutuality and shared delight.

✝

Jennifer McBride, writing about Bonhoeffer's theology of public witness, observes that for most dominant forms of American Christianity the cross functions primarily as the emblem of a doctrinal system rather than the sacrament of our conformation to Christ—as if faith were a matter of holding the right opinions.

In truth, however, in reality, Jesus' obedience, suffering, and death are not symbolic of other realities. His entire life, birth to death, was a long crucifixion, meaning that he lived and died in "the form of a sinner," in solidarity with his most desperate neighbors. And that solidarity remains, as Origen says in his Matthew commentary:

When the saints are in need of food, he also is hungry. When others of his members need medicine, he too, weak, as it were, also needs it. And when others are in need of being taken in, he himself, as if a traveler, seeks in them for where to lay his head. He thus freezes in the one who is naked and is clothed in the one who is clothed. This is why he says: I was sick and in prison and you did not visit me. For if a member of Christ is in prison, then he himself is not free of prison, for he said of the just person: I am with him in tribulation; that is, I suffer with him. For just as those who belong to me are in tribulation with me, so am I in tribulation with them.

If our faith is not a fantasy, Jesus' doings are the acts of God, constituting a new humanity, a new creation. If the Gospel is indeed gospel, Jesus, the eternal Son, the Father's and the Spirit's equal, takes on "flesh," assuming as his own our humanity, our creatureliness, infusing it with the clarity and spiritedness of his own life. As Cyril of Alexandria said, he became our "second beginning," counteracting our disobedience and undoing our abandonment. And he did this, Hebrews says, "through what he suffered."

How can that be? God is impassible, immutable. Theologically, everything depends on this truth: nothing happens to God; God happens to all things. So, what are we to make the claim that Jesus, as God, *suffered?*

Here's the staggering wonder: what Jesus experienced did not change him but was changed by him. He healed whatever he assumed—and there is nothing he has not assumed. He suffers, but, as Jenson says, he does not suffer the fact that he suffers. Nothing happens to him but what the Father wants to happen differently for us.

Jesus did not sin. He did not repent or ask to be forgiven. But in his obedience, suffering, and death, he opened up a way for us to find ourselves, to return to what it is that makes us whole. Jesus "learned obedience," but he did not become more faithful. No, thanks to what he suffered, and how he suffered it, faithfulness became possible for us. His learning was our instruction. God's law was written on our hearts by what happened in his. His "loud cries and tears" not only provoked us toward imitation but also enacted a new reality for us within the depths of our being. He entered deeply into our sorrows, into the very depths of the depths, far deeper than we can imagine, and he generated in those depths a godly sorrow, which "leads to salvation and leaves no regret," awakening in us God's own longings, "the readiness to see justice done" (2 Cor. 7:10-11).

We heard in today's Old Testament reading that God has promised to give us his own heart: "I will put my law within them, and I will write it on their hearts" (Jer. 31:33). The New Testament reading (Heb. 5:7-10) tells us that God has accomplished it, and how:

> In the days of his flesh, Jesus offered up prayers and supplications, with loud cries and tears, to the one who was able to save him from death, and he was heard because of his reverent submission. Although he was a Son, he learned obedience through what he suffered; and

having been made perfect, he became the
source of eternal salvation for all who obey him,
having been designated by God a high priest
according to the order of Melchizedek.

All to say, if we want to know as we are meant to know,
to know as we are known, we have to attend to what it
means for Jesus to have become the source of all our
good by suffering as he suffered. As we are being
perfected, we will have to offer up those same prayers
and cry those very tears.

✝

Lent, as we know, is a season of repentance. But what,
exactly, does it mean to repent? Certainly, it cannot be
reduced to feelings of guilt or unworthiness. But can it,
in fact, be done? Is justice really possible?

The Ash Wednesday liturgy in the Book of Common
Prayer includes a litany of penitence, which begins with
the confession that we've not loved as we should. It
ends with a request: "Accomplish in us the work of

your salvation that we may show forth your glory in the world." We are asking, notice, to be able to *do* something—something restorative, something life-giving, something *good*.

In response, the priest declares this absolution:

> Almighty God, the Father of our Lord Jesus Christ, who desires not the death of sinners, but rather that they may turn from their wickedness and live, has given power and commandment to his ministers to declare and pronounce to his people, being penitent, the absolution and remission of their sins. He pardons and absolves all those who truly repent, and with sincere hearts believe his holy Gospel. Therefore we beseech him to grant us true repentance and his Holy Spirit, that those things may please him which we do on this day, and that the rest of our life hereafter may be pure and holy, so that at the last we may come to his eternal joy; through Jesus Christ our Lord. Amen.

Baptism, you know, is the rite of repentance. As Jenson explains, the promise of baptism is given in "strict one-to-one correlation with the two sides of its mandate... 'Be baptized ... *for the forgiveness of your sins*; and you shall receive *the gift of the Holy Spirit.*'"

Consequently, when we are baptized, we apprehend the reality the Gospel tells us is the truth of our existence. In and by that rite we are told—so we never forget—that God has put all our old disobediences behind us, and put in us his own heart, his own strength of purpose. Every time we repent, as we do in the Ash Wednesday liturgy, as we do every Sunday in the Eucharistic liturgy, we're "remembering" that baptism—catching up, once again, to its eternal truth, opening ourselves anew to the co-inhabiting Spirit of life.

Nick Cave, the Australian singer and poet, in his recently published conversations with Seán O'Hagan, speaks of sin as forms of bad practice that weigh us down, suffocating us, so that we become less and less capable of joy, sympathy, gratitude, kindness, peace. Regret, he suggests, can help us free ourselves from the burden.

> We all have regrets and most of us know that those regrets, as excruciating as they can be, are the things that help us lead improved lives. Or, rather, there are certain regrets that, as they emerge, can accompany us on the incremental bettering of our lives. Regrets are forever floating to the surface... They require our attention. You have to do something with them. One way is to seek forgiveness by making what might be called living amends, by using whatever gifts you may have in order to help rehabilitate the world.

That is what repentance is, truly. A living amends, the slow betterment of our lives, borne along by myriad graces, leading toward the rehabilitation of the world—at least some small corners of it. Regret, rightly held, receives the grace of contrition. And contrition, as gift, makes possible the kind of repentance that heals the world.

Make no mistake: that kind of repentance is *work*. Forgiveness and renewal simply do not and cannot happen apart from our readiness to face the truth and our efforts to right the wrongs we've done or let be done. Pardon and absolution require radical and far-reaching change.

So, we should pray for the gift of tears, the grace of contrition, knowing what it is we're praying for. Graced tears, tears that arise from the depth of our heart of hearts, do not come quickly or painlessly. In the words of one of the nameless Desert Fathers, "Tears are the Promised Land. And it took forty years for the Children of Israel to enter the Promised Land."

If we are to be free of our sins, we must grieve them. We must grieve them and we must make restitution for them. We cannot manage this work on our own, needless to say. It must be *granted* to us. And thankfully, believe it or not, it *is* granted—every time we ask.

In spite of what some of us have been told, we're not forgiven because we repent; we can repent because we're forgiven. Because what is granted to us in absolution is nothing other than God himself, the Holy Spirit, the Lord and Giver of life.

When we are bold to pray the Our Father, the prayer the Lord taught us to pray, we acknowledge that God's forgiveness of us in some sense waits on our forgiveness of others. Does this mean that God's forgiveness is conditional? No, not quite. What it means is that we can receive God's forgiveness, accept it as true, only as we participate in it by granting it to others.

As Sarah Coakley has said, forgiveness is humanly impossible; only God can do it in us. But as we, in obedience and out of desire for the joy set before us, give ourselves to the work that in fact is God's, our lives are *truly* re-aligned with his, renewed, at some secret depth, by God's own liveliness. We do begin to delight in God's will and walk in God's ways. That, and nothing less than that, is what we're promised.

Repentance is work, the hardest work. But it is, at heart, work *God* is doing in us, the fruit of his life coming alive in us. Origen, in his commentary on Romans, explains it well:

A person puts to death the deeds of the flesh through the Spirit in the following manner: "The fruit of the Spirit is love," but hatred is a deed of the flesh; therefore, hatred is put to death and extinguished through love. Likewise, joy is a fruit of the Spirit, whereas "the sorrow of this world," which works death, is a deed of the flesh; therefore, this sorrow is extinguished when the joy of the Spirit is in us. Peace is a fruit of the Spirit, dissension and discord are of the flesh. But surely discord can be put to death through peace. In a similar manner, the patience of the Spirit extinguishes the impatience of the flesh, and goodness destroys malice, and gentleness ferocity, and self-control immoderation, and chastity slays unchastity. Whoever puts to death the deeds of the flesh through the Spirit in such a manner will live.

Repentance is work. But it is work that *can be done* precisely because it is the work that *must* be done for all things to be true to what Christ has made them to be. God, who is unerringly faithful, who cannot lie, always finishes the work he has started. This, remember, was the root of Paul's apostolic joy: "Being confident of this very thing, that he which hath begun a good work in you will perform it until the day of Jesus Christ" (Phil. 2:6).

It's impossible to overstate how good God is. And it is impossible to exaggerate how devoted God is to our becoming good—with his own goodness.

Repentance is work—God's work, which works in and upon and through our doings. Precisely for that reason, it is always rewarded—and then some. As St Athanasius says, it would have been unfitting for God to leave us at the mercy of our sins, to let death have the last word over us, and it would be unworthy of God merely to restore what had been lost through the Fall. Sin takes from us our freedom, our natural humanity. What God gives us, forgiving our sins, is exceedingly, abundantly *more*—God's own freedom, God's own humanity.

✝

"This life has been given to you for repentance; do not waste it..." St Isaac the Syrian said that in one of his sermons (Homily 74). In another, later sermon (Homily 32), however, he warns his hearers that the work of repentance cannot be fully completed in this life. So, finally (in Homily 51), he urges them to be courageous in their penitence—to repent more boldly than they've sinned.

For St Isaac, repentance is the second grace, the regeneration of the new life given in baptism. It is, he says, the door to mercy, opened to all who knock at it, the mother of life that gives birth to joy. And so, he prays for God to open his heart, to "make smooth the path of repentance" in him, to deem him worthy "to taste the delight of the gift of repentance," the deep contrition inside which the gift of pure prayer is hidden like a pearl.

Martha Reeves (who writes as Maggie Ross), the Anglican solitary, has said that repentance, more than anything else, is about being restored to ourselves. She presses us to think of the pain of contrition, the sorrowing that comes as we take suffering to heart— especially the suffering we have caused *God*—, as holy pain. It is holy, she says, because it is a sign that God is indeed returning us to ourselves and to one another, reestablishing us in our rightful place as his children, his friends, his partners by restoring in us the purity of our being.

In that knowledge, given by the light of Lent, confident we can trust ourselves to God and to God's repair, we can pray much as St Isaac did:

> O Lord Jesus Christ,
> my flesh-and-bone God,
> You wept over Lazarus—
> let me weep over you.
> Your side was riven—
> let me give birth to contrition.
>
> Let your head, bowed in death,
> lift up my head.

Let your brow, crowned with blood,
purify my thoughts.
Let your face, bruised and spat upon,
brighten my eyes.
Let your mouth, filled with gall,
fill my mouth with songs.
Let your hands, stretched out in death,
teach my hands to war.
Let your feet, nailed to the tree,
guide me in the paths of peace.

By your passion, cure my passions.
By your wounds, wound my heart.
By your blood, cleanse my desires.

I forsake you, O Lord, again and again.
Do not forsake me.
I'm a sheep lost in the wilds—bear me
home in your arms.
Feed me by the still waters of your mysteries.
Hide me in the shelter of your heart, the secret
place of the Most High. That I may become
worthy of the way you see me.

O my Jesus, make my heart a home
for your holy family, a throne for you
and your Mother, and for all
with whom you long to share it.
Now and unto the ages of ages.
Amen.

7

Transfiguring
Being

A Sermon for Palm Sunday
Isaiah 50:4-9; Psalm 31:9-16; Philippians 2:5-11; Mark 14:1-15:47

Wim Wenders' *The Salt of the Earth*, a bio-doc about the photographer and photojournalist Sebastião Salgado, opens with images Salgado made of the Serra Pelada ("Naked Mountain") gold mine in Brazil, and the sounds of Salgado's reflections on his experience.

We first see the photographer's stunning black-and-white images, then his face reflected on the photographs themselves, while we listen to his mesmerizing narration:

> When I reached the edge of that enormous hole, every hair on my body stood on end. I'd never seen anything like it. Here, in a split second, I saw unfolding before me the history of mankind. The building of the pyramids. The tower of Babel. The mines of King Solomon. Not the sound of a single machine could be heard. All you could hear was the babble of 50,000 people in one huge hole. Conversations, noises, human sounds mingled with the sounds of manual labor. I had returned to the dawn of time. I could almost hear the gold whispering in the souls of these men...

The images are overwhelming. And the description, at least at first, only intensifies the confusion. When Zoë, my daughter, and I first saw the film, we could not figure out what it was that we were seeing or how it related to what was being said about these thousands upon thousands of mud-caked bodies swarming in this enormous wound in the mountainside.

Eventually, it became clear, and when it did, the images somehow seemed even more mysterious.

> All this earth had to be removed. It's not all gold. The guys had to climb small ladders, leading to bigger ones, to emerge at the top. All these men together formed an extremely organized world but in complete madness. You get the impression they're slaves, but there wasn't a single slave. They were only slaves to the idea of getting rich. Everybody wanted to get rich. There were all sorts: intellectuals, university graduates, farm employees, urban workers—people from all walks of life were trying their luck. Because when you'd hit a vein of gold everyone working that little section of the mine had the right to choose one sack. And in that sack that they chose—and this is the slavery aspect—there might be nothing… or a kilo of gold! At that very moment one's freedom

was at stake. Men who come into contact with
gold can never leave it.

Something similar happens to us today, I believe, on
Palm Sunday, at the end of Lent and at the beginning
of Holy Week. As we hear the passion narrative from
Mark's Gospel, we're made witnesses of a witness,
confronted by the mystery of an experience that is not
ours but nonetheless somehow involves us. Contact
with Christ is not like contact with gold, however. As
the Gospel stories make clear, contact with Christ
heals.

✝

We're familiar with the story of the Passion, of course.
At least its broad strokes. Historically speaking, we
know what happened. Liturgically speaking, we know
what is going to happen in the coming days—the
jubilant entry to the city; the clearing of the temple; the
last supper; the agony in the garden; the betrayal and
arrest; the trials; the condemnation; the crucifixion;
the burial. Still, we need this liturgical cycle to return us

again and again to this story precisely because we do not yet know what we need to know the way we need to know it. Repentance, as the Desert Fathers insisted, is a never-finished work.

Bad readings of Scripture leave us with the impression that what happened to Jesus in Jerusalem was obviously shameful, almost a sham, as if those caught up in the doing of it were acting in bad faith or possessed by evil spirits. This is precisely the impression that Mel Gibson creates in his *Passion of the Christ*. And our sermons, if we're not careful, leave some of that impression, too. But the Gospels tell a much more troubling story.

No matter what we've heard, the Passion is not The Greatest Story Ever Told, not the Last Battle between Good and Evil. It's the unfolding of everyday petty jealousies; religious fervor and political savvy; predictable crowd dynamics and all-too-familiar fear of the police; common cruelty; common cowardice; confusion and uncertainty; and, most of all, stupidity.

St. Paul says that if the rulers of this world had known what they were doing, "they would not have crucified the Lord of glory" (1 Cor. 2:8).

It's easy to overlook the fact that almost nothing is said about evil or the diabolic in the passion narratives. Jesus' arrest, trials, and execution—remember, those are the terms the authorities want us to use (instead of words like rape, torture, and murder)—happened naturally, not supernaturally.

This is especially surprising and all the more revealing in the Gospel of Mark, which from the first focuses on Jesus' conflict with Satan and the demons.

At the beginning of the Gospel, he defeats Satan in the wilderness. And he drives out whatever unclean spirits he encounters on his journey to Jerusalem. But once he has reached the city, he falls into the hands of powerful men—their agendas, their ambitions, their fear of the mob. And everyone else, including those who love him best, find themselves at a loss about what to do to save him.

Just so, the Gospel confronts us with a terrifying truth: Jesus' life ended as it did, not because the powers of evil overcame him, still less because God forced it to happen for the sake of accomplishing a predetermined "plan." No, Jesus' life ended as it did because ordinary human beings, including the faithful and loving and hopeful ones, could not imagine an alternative to the injustice they found themselves enacting.

We need to feel the weight of this fact. People condemned Jesus, and required his death, or failed even to try to save him from his sufferings, not because they despised him but because they were so afraid of their own death or the end of their way of life that they could not see what was happening to him as anything but unavoidable. A few, perhaps, gloated in Jesus' sufferings. Some, no doubt, wanted to see the end of his ministry. But most, I'm sure, admired him, or at least regarded him with respect. Why, then, do they accept his death without protest?

It's not hard to imagine what the ordinary folk in the city and the outlying towns must have said to one

127

another after they heard the news. I can see them shaking their heads in disbelief: "It's too bad, really. I'm no fan of Pilate or Herod or Caiaphas, as you know. But at the end of the day, what else were they going to do?" "It's not right. It's not right. But he did push it too far, didn't he?" "We should've said something, done something. But what?"

Not everyone cried, "Crucify him!" But did anyone cry, "Don't crucify him"? Judas was paid to betray him. But did anyone try to buy his release? Not everyone forsook him. Not everyone that passed by him on the cross mocked him. But did anyone cry out to God for his deliverance?

No doubt, some in the circles of power, like Nicodemus and Joseph of Arimathea, did not agree to Jesus's condemnation. But even they seem to have been more or less resigned to his fate. Those outside the circles of power, including his disciples and his family, surely felt something of that same helplessness. Peter was not the only disciple to deny him.

That helplessness, that reluctance to resist injustices, that sense of the inevitability of evil that we hear whispering through this story and its silences is the "slavery aspect" of sin, exposed by the miseries and mysteries of God's passion.

✝

Today's Old Testament reading, and the Psalm, speak in the first person. We are meant to hear them in Jesus' voice. *He* is the one who says, "I gave my back to those who struck me, and my cheek to those who pulled out the beard." *He* is the one who says, "Have mercy on me, O Lord, for I am in trouble... I have become a reproach to all my enemies and even to my neighbors."

So read, these texts witness to the mystery of the incarnation. As I've said several times now—nothing happens to God; God happens to all things. That happening is what makes all things what they are.

As a result, in becoming "flesh" God alters reality from within its deepest center, its innermost depths, opening it up fully to God and so giving it his essence as its own fulness. Jesus, the Word, does not become a human being, one more among the many, but assumes to himself humanity itself.

He is, we confess, human in every way that we are, except for sin. But he is not simply another one of us, a number out of the number that no man can number. He is God, the Word. Taking on our creatureliness, he, as Son, creates a relation to the Father through the Spirit for us. That relation is our being, our being human.

The apostolic witness returns again and again to one version or another of the claim that Jesus is the one in whom all that God is, and all that creation is and can be, are joined—joined and conjoined.

In him, all good opposites are made to coincide. In him, all rivalry and conflict are overcome. "All things have been created through him and for him," Paul says. "He himself is before all things, and in him all things hold together" (Col. 1:16-17).

Later in that same letter, "You have died, and your life is hidden with Christ in God." Therefore, Paul concludes, you have this particular hope: "When Christ who is your life is revealed, then you will also be revealed with him in glory" (Col. 3:3-4).

The hope that Paul shares with the Colossians he knows because of his own mystical experience of Christ—an experience he had not known to hope for:

> I have been crucified with Christ, and it is no longer I who live, but it is Christ who lives in me. And the life I now live in the flesh I live by faith in the Son of God, who loved me and gave himself for me. (Gal. 2:19-20).

Today's New Testament reading calls us to share that same hope, and to stand in awe of the unthinkable goodness of it:

> Let the same mind be in you that was in Christ Jesus, who, though he was in the form of God, did not regard equality with God as something to be exploited,

but emptied himself,
taking the form of a slave,
being born in human likeness.
And being found in human form,
he humbled himself and became obedient
to the point of death–even death on a cross.
Therefore God also highly exalted him
and gave him the name
that is above every name,
so that at the name of Jesus
every knee should bend,
in heaven and on earth and under the earth,
and every tongue should confess
that Jesus Christ is Lord,
to the glory of God the Father. (Phil. 2:5-11)

As you know, this passage can be and often is taken to mean that Jesus had to give up "the form of God" in order to be found in human form. But no. That reading wrongly assumes a competition between God's being and ours. As if for Jesus to take on our likeness he had to disfigure himself. As if he had to change his relation to God in order to make a relationship with God possible for us.

The incarnation changes nothing for him, for God. Nothing. The incarnation is not an interruption in God's life as Trinity. The incarnation is not a humiliation for the Son or a correction for the Father.

Nothing is more fitting than for God to be human. If that were not so, then the incarnation would not and could not be the revelation of God—or our salvation.

Christ's "kenosis," then, should not be understood as an emptying out, or a jettisoning of his divinity. It is, instead, a filling up of our humanity, which he takes as his own. Not a negation of anything—a *fulfilling*.

Jesus does not "scale down" his divinity in order to make his humanity viable. His humanity is viable precisely because it is fully open to his fulfilling communion with the Father by the Spirit.

Taking on flesh, God the Word does not empty himself of his fullness, but in his fullness descends into the emptiness of our existence and fills it with himself, saving us from emptiness.

This is the critical point: becoming "obedient to the point of death, even death on a cross," Jesus, the Son, did not alter himself or his Father in the least, did not become less or other than he always was and is and shall be. He became what we are without ceasing to be who he is.

In him, the divine neither recedes nor dominates and the human is neither diminished nor overwhelmed. Taking on humanity, he is not stripped of his dignity as God; instead, he dignifies us, exalting our nature, revealing that a slave, even a criminal slave, is no less human, no less worthy of honor, than a lord. As St. Anselm says, "In the incarnation of God it is understood that no humiliation of God came about: rather it is believed that human nature was exalted."

The wonder is that Jesus, the Beloved, not only shares with us what is his, but also includes us in who he is. He identifies with us so completely that he cannot be known apart from us anymore than he can be known apart from the Father. And because of what he suffered and how he suffered it, we can partake in his life and in his death, not merely imitating his example but sharing his experiences, co-existing with him, so that no line can be drawn between his being for us and our being with him.

We can come to know Christ, as St Paul did, in the "the power of his resurrection and participation in his sufferings, becoming like him in his death, and so, somehow, attaining to the resurrection from the dead" (Phil. 3:10). And we can come to partner with him in his charge, completing the mission he has given us to do. That, nothing less, is the promise of Holy Week: not only recalling what happened to Jesus, not only giving thanks for the victory of God accomplished through his sufferings, but also becoming the kind of people who can live his life as he lived and lives it, working the works of God.

God does not begrudge us our existence, St Athanasius says. That's hard for us to believe, isn't it? But it's true—truer than we're able to imagine. God would rather not be God at all than to be God apart from us, without us.

God not only wants good for us, and only ever good; God wants *everything* good for us, for each and every last one of us.

God wants us not as servants but as friends, not as heirs but as *joint*-heirs.

Perhaps you think that all sounds too good to be true, too supportive, too generous. Or perhaps you think it sounds outright indulgent, unfitting for God. If so, then listen to what St Maximus says:

> This is the mystery which circumscribes all the ages, and which reveals the grand plan of God, a super-infinite plan infinitely pre-existing the ages an infinite number of times. The essential Word of God became a messenger of this plan when He became man, and, if I may rightly say so, revealed Himself as the innermost depth of the Father's goodness while also displaying in

Himself the very goal for which creatures manifestly received the beginning of their existence. And this is because it is for the sake of Christ—that is, for the whole mystery of Christ—that all the ages and the beings existing within those ages received their beginning and end in Christ.

God promises to be all in all. That is why we exist. That is why there is something rather than nothing. What is in store for us is the transfiguration of all things, the transfiguration of being itself.

In that transfiguration, not one good thing will be lost. Indeed, as Jordan Daniel Wood has said, commenting on St Maximus' vision of the creation's fulfillment, God, precisely in order to save "even the most apparently incidental attribute of every last created being, must really *be* all things." Not just *in* all things. But in them as he is in himself. According to Eriugena, "all things shall be converted into God as the air into light." Or, as Jenson says, "the end is music."

Hearing that, we should ask Nicodemus' question—
and Mary's: "How can this be?"

It will happen because God will make it happen.
Indeed, God is *already* making it happen. As Simon
Tugwell puts it in his little book on prayer, the Lord, as
Spirit, is able to "get hold" of us, working "below the
level of our deliberate control." He can "hook" us—
remember, Tugwell says, he *is* a fisherman—"so that,
even though we may kick and scream and try to get
away, he will at the end be able to land us safely at his
feet."

But because there is no rivalry between God's being
and doing and ours, and because our existence is co-
extensive and co-determined, the transfiguration of all
things happens because *we* make it happen. Creation,
remember, groans in longing for *our* manifestation as
sons in the Son (Rom. 8:19-21).

Because God's happening makes us, we can make that
happening happen for others. We can, St Paul told the
Philippians, work out our salvation because—and only

because—God is at work in and among us (Phil. 2:12-13). Because God is—so gladly!—at work in us, happening to us, *our* love, born of his pleasure, overflows—and changes the world (Phil. 1:9-11).

✝

Earlier, in this morning's Liturgy of the Palms, we heard the story of Christ's so-called Triumphal Entry (Mk 11:1-11). In Mark's telling, Jesus, outside Jerusalem, sends two disciples to find a colt for him: "If anyone says to you, 'Why are you doing this?' just say this: 'The Lord needs it and will send it back here immediately'" (Mk 11:3).

These are pregnant lines. Christ, of course, as God, needs nothing. But he cannot be human, cannot share our being, cannot be what we need him to be except by taking on our neediness—and by making himself dependent on our care. To come, Christ must *borne*.

There is only one "gate of the Lord" (Ps. 118:20). That is Jesus. But in him we are ourselves "the gates of righteousness" (Ps. 118:19). He is for us the Gate precisely because he makes *us* gates—openings in the fabric of history for him to enter, not imperially, but modestly, "lowly and riding on a donkey" (Zech. 9:9). Mary's song tells us the truth, the same truth we find in the Beatitudes: the lowlier we are, the more room we make for his appearing.

The final chapters of Tugwell's book are given to reflections on our growth in freedom and the coming of the Kingdom of God. We are meant to be, in the words of the Apostle Paul, "the fullness of him who fills all in all" (Eph. 1:23). We can become that fullness, however, only as we give ourselves over completely in Christ to the Father through the Spirit—not in servility but with authority. We are, as Tugwell says, to be docile. But docility to *God* is true freedom. That is why the culminating fruit of the Spirit's work in our lives is *self*-control.

We are not meant to "patch up" the world, to fix ourselves or our neighbors. We are meant to rule with Christ as his co-equal co-regents. And that reign begins now, here, not so much "breaking in" as "peeking through," as we take responsibility for what is happening in our corner of the world, as we take to heart the sufferings of our neighbors.

Christ is born—and borne—into the world right at the point of our needs, met and unmet, and our meeting of our neighbors' needs.

✝

In *The Salt of the Earth*, Salgado recounts his time with the Saraguro people in Ecuador. He says he learned from one of them, Lupe, that according to their legends, "God, in the image of Christ, was to return to earth to observe them to decide who'd go to heaven." Lupe was convinced Salgado was Christ. "He seriously believed that I'd come as a special observer to report 'up there' about their behavior."

Later in the film, Salgado recalls his time among the Coptic Christians in the Sahal region of Africa during the famine. He remarks on their humility, how they would not cut in line for food or water, even if they were carrying a dying child. He explains how they died not from starvation, but from parallel diseases after their bodies had been weakened by malnutrition and dehydration.

Seeing these images, hearing these stories, I could not help but grieve that after all this time most of us who identify as Christians have still not understood that we *are* the image of Christ—not called to observe others, deciding who goes to heaven, but serving them, caring for them, delighting in them.

Palm Sunday is a reminder that God is always working, doing what only God can do. And because it shows us Jesus, the theandric one, it is also a reminder that we are called to join in that always-ongoing work, working the works of God, the works we were created to do, the works prepared for us from the foundation of the worlds.

We're not meant to remain witnesses of the witness of Christ's entry. We're meant to take him in, to receive him with joy, so we're transfigured by the mystery of his coming. As Rahner says:

> What took place in the very depths of reality (whether we realize it or not) through the incarnation of the Son, his death and his resurrection, may be rendered present to the spirit of man also through the word of his messengers, and may be received in a spirit of obedience and faith into the very center of man himself, into that dimension in which he is free to be whoever he will be, and so who he ought to be.

You are meant to be free. Free to live life as you long to live it. This, nothing less, is what God prayed and prays for us, for you, to know. And God's prayers are sure to be answered. Indeed, they already have been. God wants you to live your life. That's why he gave you his.

So, I leave with this assurance: I can hear something whispering in your souls, a hum lower than all other sounds, the mystery of your faith. Christ has died;

Christ is risen; therefore go, *be*—transfigured. And as you go, let these words from St Ephrem burn in your heart:

> Our King comes in majestic glory.
> Let us light our lamps
> and go forth to meet Him.
> Let us find our joy in Him,
> for He has found joy in us.
> He will indeed rejoice us
> with His marvelous light.
> Amen.

Made in the USA
Monee, IL
12 April 2023